James Newton Matthews

Tempe Vale

And Other Poems

James Newton Matthews

Tempe Vale
And Other Poems

ISBN/EAN: 9783744704816

Printed in Europe, USA, Canada, Australia, Japan

Cover: Foto ©Thomas Meinert / pixelio.de

More available books at **www.hansebooks.com**

TEMPE VALE

—AND—

OTHER POEMS

—BY—

JAMES NEWTON MATTHEWS

The songs of dead seasons, that wander
On wings of articulate words;
Lost leaves that the shore-wind may squander,
Light flocks of untamable birds;
Some sang to me dreaming in class-time,
And truant in hand as in tongue;
For the youngest were born of boy's pastime,
The eldest are young.
                    SWINBURNE.

CHICAGO
CHARLES H. KERR & COMPANY
175 DEARBORN STREET
1888

Copyright, 1888
By James N. Matthews

DEDICATION.

TO THE

MEMORY OF MY FATHER & MOTHER,

AND TO

MY FAIREST CRITIC, MY WIFE,

This little book is lovingly inscribed.

J. N. M.

CONTENTS.

	PAGE.
PROEM—*The Spirit of Poetry*,	9
Tempe Vale,	11
A Legend Beautiful,	15
The City of Snow,	16
A Dream of Beauty,	17
The Death of the Baby,	19
November Down the Wabash,	21
The Old Mill,	23
Alone at the Farm,	26
Her Knitting Needles,	28
To the March Moon,	30
A Dream,	32
A Sea-weed,	33
There is no Luck about the House,	35
Genius,	37
A Nocturne,	38
My Guest,	40
A Vision,	44
The First Gray Hair,	45
Edison,	47
The Vale of Gold,	49
The Crime,	51
March,	53
She Sleeps,	54
'Way Down in Spice Valley,	57
A Fragment,	60

CONTENTS.

	PAGE.
The Old House-fly,	61
Insomnia,	66
They had no Poet and so They Died,	67
At Waterloo,	69
Gaun Hame,	70
A Ballad of Tears,	71
July in the West.	73
Illinois,	75
The Eyes of Eleanora,	78
O, Bleak is the Night,	80
A Burden of Babylon,	82
Behind the Veil,	83
Day and Night,	86
One Golden Hair,	87
In Summer Woods,	89
Severed Friendship,	91
My Lady Beautiful,	93
In Soudan,	94
Out on the Farm,	95
The Old Fire-place,	96
Joukydaddles,	100
To a Terrapin,	102
A Profile of Fall,	104
A Valentine,	107
'Tis Always Sunday in the Woods,	108
Lines in an Album,	110
When Your Father went to War,	111
An Invocation,	118
A Ballade of Busy Doctors,	120
Goodnight and Joy be with you All,	122
Shakespeare,	124
The Soldier of Castile,	126
Her Feet on the Fender,	131
The Old Village Depot,	133
Indian Summer,	136
Lady Laura in the North,	139

CONTENTS.

	PAGE.
Meadows of Gold,	142
At Uncle Reuben Ragan's,	144
The Night you Quoted Burns to Me,	148
The Mystery of Barrington Meadows,	150
When I am Old,	154
The Passing of the Old Year,	156
An Extravagant Simile,	157
The Pioneers,	159
Taking in the Hammock,	169
At Christmas Eve,	170
The Old Major Speaks,	171
A Garland for the Dead,	174
The Foolish Mariners,	177

SONNETS AND RONDEAUX.

To a Sleeping Boy,	183
A Night in June,	184
When I Come Home,	185
At Milking Time,	186
October,	187
November,	188
Where Willie Was,	189
In Days to Come,	190
Christmas Morning,	191
Doom,	192
Rondeaux of Remembrance,	193
John A. Warder,	195
A Bluebird in January,	196
Could She but Know,	197
Could Love do More,	198
My Favorite Poem,	199
What is Death,	200

THE SPIRIT OF POETRY.

*She steers the stars through Heaven's azure deep;
She lifts the leaden eyelids of the morn;
On distant hills she winds the hunter's horn,
And wakes the lonely shepherd from his sleep;
She scales the dizzy ledge where torrents leap,
And hangs the bloom upon the bristling thorn;
She sits for hours in solitudes forlorn,
With downcast eyes, where hapless lovers weep.
When Spring comes up the vale in Winter's trace,
She plucks the blossom from the bud's embrace;
She binds the golden girdle round the bee,
And lends the lily's luster to the pea;
She curves the swallow's wing, and guides its flight,
And tips the dewy meads with twinkling light.*

She rides, she revels on the rushing storm,
  She suns her pinions on the rainbow's rim—
  She laves in mountain pools her snowy limb,
As sweetly chaste as Dian and as warm;
In summer fields she bares her blushing arm,
  And sings among the reapers. By the dim
  Light of autumnal moons, her tresses swim
On gales Lethean, with assuasive charm.
Into the chamber of the alchemist
  She peers, or, through some half-closed lattice, sees
Her lover by the wanton night wind kissed.
  Anon, she walks the dim Hesperides,
Or, mingling with the spirits of the mist,
  Dances at will along the darkling seas.

IN TEMPE VALE.

In Tempe vale the sun shines fair,
   O'er crystal streams forever flowing,—
On Tempe's rainbow-girdled air
   The velvet-breasted flowers are blowing
And up the valley, everywhere,
   The golden orange groves are glowing:—
And violets uplift their eyes,
Bewildered, to the stooping skies,
Dreaming all day of Paradise;
   And blue-bells from the tufted sod,
When darkness down Olympus dies,
   Out-stretch their pearly palms to God,
And pour their fragrant sacrifice,
And all the world is in a trance
Along Peneus' blue expanse,
         In Tempe vale.

In Tempe vale, no sound of wars
Goes ever to the mild-eyed stars;
No lily's breast is tinged with blood,
   No dreamer from his rest is driven,
But ever from the drowsy wood,
   There floateth to the jeweled heaven

Eternal lullabies, like those
That murmur in the crimson rose;
   Or like the symphonies that break
   From out some lone enchanted lake;
Or like the rhapsodies that quiver,
By night, along some sacred river,—
   Ah, only holiest things of earth,
   Spring into beauty, and to birth
          In Tempe vale.

In Tempe vale no bough is stirred,
   No winds are in the conscious tree;
The only melodies there heard—
Except the trill of some wild bird,
   Or tumult of the tippling bee—
   Are those dim strains of minstrelsy
That tingle to the twilight stars,
From laughing lutes and low guitars,
   On many a Grecian lover's knee;
And dark-eyed maids, with lips of wine,
And limbs of snow, their tresses twine,
   By fountains flashing from the hills,
   And all the golden ether spills
A summer splendor 'round the vine,
          In Tempe vale.

In Tempe vale, in Tempe's bowers,
   The soul, intoxicate with bliss,
Goes reeling through a world of flowers
   That hath no counterpart in this;
And far beneath the lote-tree's shade,
   Where glow-worms glimmer in the grass,
Is heard the lonely serenade
Of some heart-broken nightingale;
   And dew-drops, like a sea of glass,
Their love-lights up the valley trail,
   Until the night-tide shadows pass,
And daylight dawns o'er Tempe vale,
        O'er Tempe vale.

In Tempe vale, they weave the dance,
   Along its lone, star-lighted river,
By those wild grottos of romance
   O'er which the mellow citrons quiver,
   And laughing love lives on forever!
Ah, nightly to the cithern's sigh,
The Muses, from their haunts on high,
   Come tripping hither, every one,—
   And Pan, and young Endymion,
And Dian, with her dapper crew,
   The piping shepherd-lads, and all

The Dryads o'er the mountain wall,
Come thronging to the revel, too,
        In Tempe vale.

To Tempe vale, a long good-night!
  The glamour of my idle dream
Is over-past. My waking sight,
  Alas! is blinded to the gleam
And beauty of that valley bright.
Its blissful bowers no more I see,
  Its peaceful paths have passed from view,
Yet down to the Ægean Sea,
  Still fall its winding waters blue,
Still sings the bird, and hums the bee
  In every nook the dreamer knew.
No summer-poet's fickle thought,
On Fancy's pinions ever sought
A spot with sweeter raptures fraught,
        Than Tempe vale.

A LEGEND BEAUTIFUL.

'Twas thus the Dervish spake: "Upon our right,
   There stands, unseen, an angel with a pen,
   Who notes down each good deed of ours, and then
Seals it with kisses in the Master's sight.
Upon our left a sister-angel sweet
   Keeps daily record of each evil act,
But, great with love, folds not the mournful sheet
   Till deepest midnight, when, if conscience-racked,
We lift to Allah our repentant hands,
She smiles and blots the record where she stands;
But if we seek not pardon for our sin,
She seals it with a tear, and hands it in."

THE CITY OF SNOW.

Silently, silently, all the night,
   Out in the fields, where the north winds blow,
A shimmering army, robed in white,
   Is building the City of Snow.

Hour after hour, their task they ply,
   Down where the roses used to grow,
Piling the battlements steep and high
   Of the silent City of Snow.

Out in the dark in the driving storm,
   To and fro, they glimmer and glow,
All night, as their deft hands frame and form
   The mystic City of Snow.

Never the sound of a hammer smites
   The milk-white silence, above or below,
And dumber than dreams are the dapper sprites,
   That build the City of Snow.

'Tis morn! and the labor is all complete,
   And the cold north wind has ceased to blow,
And Vandal feet are abroad in the street
   Of the sinless City of Snow.

A DREAM OF BEAUTY.

I

I muse on her dark eyes, and see the gloss
  Of dewy grapes that purple in the gloom
Of amorous gardens, where the faint winds toss
  O'er violet reaches, panting with perfume;
A dream of fawns! peering with passionate glance
  Between the lindens, at mid-summer dawn,
  When love awakens, and desire is on,
And piping robins hold the world in trance.

II

I dream of her dark hair, and feel the dusk
  Of cooling myrtles, in the twilight vales
Of Tempe, when no mellowing moonbeams husk
  The shadows from the shifting nightingales;
A vision of swift ravens, heading south
  Between pomegranate boughs, amidst the hills
  Of Arcady, what time the summer spills
Its kindling kisses on the lily's mouth.

III

I sing of her white hands — two dimpled sprites
  More tremulous, and stainless, and more soft
Than rose-leaves opening in mid-summer nights,
  By moon-dawns, in the deepest woodland croft;
A vision of vain hopes! a shimmering mist
  Of swan-down, cincturing each lovely limb
  Of Mab's hand-maidens, when the warm stars trim
Their dewy tresses with pale amethyst.

IV

Then, fancying her love, I hear the coo
  Of doves, far-hidden in the citron groves
Of Hellas, where the high gods came to woo,
  And change for mortal, their immortal loves;
A vision of the ripening south — a dream
  Of loveliness and passion, song and wine,
  And Greek girls lolling where the Bacchanal vine
Tipples and sips the summer's amber beam.

THE DEATH OF THE BABY.

I

Like a bird flying out of its prison,
    Light-winged and alone,
The soul of wee Robbie is risen,
    And heavenward flown.

II

Flown heavenward out of its anguish,
    Sweet motherless one!
Flown heavenward never to languish,
    As time weareth on.

III

As out of a lily's pale chalice
    The odor is blown,
So, forth from the soul's snowy palace,
    The life-light is gone.

IV

As soft as the tinges of twilight
    Out-fade from the west,
The baby sank into the skylight
    Of infinite rest.

V

No longer his pink baby-fingers
    Outrival the flowers,
No longer his baby-laugh lingers,
    And melts into ours.

VI

The cradle is empty and hollow,
    Forever and aye,
The flight of wee Robbie we'll follow,
    When beckoned away.

NOVEMBER DOWN THE WABASH.

Upon the Wabash hills, and down
The lonesome glens, the leaves are brown
With early frost, and gray birds skim
The cooling waters, and the slim
Ungartered willows stand, knee-deep
Along the river's edge, and weep
To see the Summer's parting gleam
Pass, like a shadow, down the stream,
Or like the memory of one
We loved in youth, and doted on.

Silence is on the Wabash hills,
Save where a lonely blue-bird trills
Upon the windy oak, or where
The nuts drip from the branches bare,
Or squirrels chatter in the sun; —
A hush, as if all life were done,
Reigns thro' the woods; the waters lie
So dead and motionless, the sky
Leans dolorously down, as though
To meet its mirrored self below.

No boyish laughter pours along
The Wabash hills,—no lover's song
Re-echoes up the tangled ways,
As in the long, glad summer days;
No bare-foot lads, with hook and rod,
Beside the shadowy waters plod,—
No maids come down to twine and strew
With valley-flowers, the old canoe,—
Only a blind owl floating by,
And far clouds driving up the sky.

Thus, like a sombre shadow, broods
November, o'er the Wabash woods;
Far to the south, the slanting sun
Has gone, and Winter soon will run
His sledges up the frozen heights,—
And grates will glow, and long dark nights
Will trance the drowsy brain with dreams
Of other days,—and fitful gleams
Of Beauty will dissolve the gloom
In seas of summer warmth and bloom.

THE OLD MILL.

The morning rose bright on the clover-clad
    hill,
  And lightly the breezes went by,
As I took the old path leading down to the
    mill,
  That stood where the bluffs beetle high;
The path leading down by the steep to the
    strand,
  Where I loitered a lad in my mirth,
When life was a beautiful rainbow that
    spanned
  The loveliest valley of earth.

The blue-bird still swung on the sycamore
    boughs,
  The sand-piper rode on the wave,
And still to the pebble-paved ford came the
    cows,
  At the noonday, to drink and to lave;
The dam was nigh down, yet the cataract fell
  O'er the ledge, with a plunge and a roar,
That seemed to my heart, in its tumult, to tell
  Of the halcyon summers of yore.

The rock was still there, where we dived in
    the tide,
  And the sands where we stretched in the
    sun,
But the many gay fellows that played at our
    side,
  Had gone from the valley, each one;
The old fishing-log it had floated away,
  And over the crumbling canoe,
The paddles were locked, in a dream of decay
  Where the mold and the rank mosses grew.

By the dust-girdled doorway, where gabbled
    the geese,
  And the pilfering swine used to stray,
The grass had grown up in an emerald fleece,
  That lovingly mantled the way;
I saw not the brown little bare-footed maid
  Trip down the long path to the spring,
I heard not the sound of her song in the glade,
  Nor the light-hearted laugh at the swing.

The mill was as mute as the miller who lies
  In his green-curtained cot on the hill,—

And I thought, as the tears gathered into my
    eyes,
　That the dead had come back to the mill;
That I saw the old wagons roll up with their
    grist,
　And again heard the rumble and roar
Of the wheels,—but, alas! it was only a mist
　Falling over my senses,—no more!

Ah, the dust-covered miller! near twenty long
    years
　Have flown, since he took his last toll;
His heart, when he died, was as sound as his
    burrs,
　And as white as his flour, was his soul;
Still the wraith of him stands at the low
    batten-door,
　And his laughter comes back from the past;
Still the sound of his footstep is heard on the
    floor,
　Tho' the mill's but a wreck in the blast.

ALONE AT THE FARM.

(*Easter.*)

As I sit alone in the twilight gray,
   Under the sound of the April rain,
My thoughts go back to an Easter day
   Of the long-ago, and I listen again,
        (But listen in vain!)
For the shouts of the boys who used to swarm
   Out of the neighboring town, like plagues,
To spend a glorious day at the farm,
   With the boys of the country, *coloring eggs*.

And I, poor fool! was as gruff as a bear,
   For I never could stand their noise—but Jane,
Sweet soul! she always welcomed them there,
   With a love that her dear heart could not feign—
      (And the boys loved Jane!)

And many a time I heard her say
   (In the after-years ere she paled and died)
That, God permitting, on Easter Day,
   She would clasp their hands on the other side.

So the years went by, and the boys were grown,
   And the grass waved high in the orchard lane,—
And down where the sounds of war were blown,
   The lads of the Easter-time lay slain;
            And oh, the pain!
And oh, the sobbing—the ceaseless moan—
   The long sad nights, and the vigils vain,
Of an old man drooping and dreaming alone,
   Of days that never come back again!

HER KNITTING NEEDLES.

In the bureau's bottom drawer, as I rum-
    maged there to-day,
  With the memory of other times aglow;
I found the knitting needles that my mother
    tucked away,
  In the twilight of a winter long ago,
They were tangled in the fingers of a wee, un-
    finished glove,
  And when I stooped and touched them, it
    did seem,
I could see the vanished features of the one
    I used to love,
  In the cheery chimney-corner of my dream.

O, the little shining lances! how they glittered
    in the light,
  Of the cabin where my mother used to sit,
In her cosy, cushioned rocker, till the middle
    of the night,
  A-crooning tender ditties as she knit;

And I feel my feet grow warmer, as I plod
 across the past,
  In the stockings that her white and holy
   hands
In their feebleness had fashioned, ere she fell
 asleep at last,
  And was borne into the summer-litten lands.

No trophies ever dangled in a mediæval hall
 More sacred for the memories they hold,
Than these, the lowly relics of the saint that I
 recall,
 Thro' the twilight of the tender days of old:
Each needle is a talisman, a token, a delight,
 A wand that lures my fancy unaware,
From the prison of the present, and its shadow
 infinite,
  To my cabin home, and mother knitting
   there.

TO THE MARCH MOON.

O moon of March! what seest thou
   But dead leaves, still? No bursting bud
Breaks into bloom on any bough,
   In all the bare, unbreathing wood.
       O sweet March moon!
Canst thou not woo the bloomy brood
   To don their kirtles, pink and white,
And, in the upland solitude,
   Come out to-night, come out to-night?

O moon of March! come down, come down,
   Perchance a new Endymion lies
On yonder hill, by yonder town,
   With peerless lips, and perfect eyes.
       O fair March moon!
Forsake the dull eternal skies,
   For just a hasty swallow-flight,
In answer to a lover's cries,—
   Come down to-night, come down to-night.

O moon of March! O lady moon,
   High-throned above the wreathing mist!

TO THE MARCH MOON.

Come down, in silver silken shoon,
    Come down with starlight round thy wrist,
        O pale March moon!
What tho' no shepherd keep his tryst,
    Like that sweet lad on Latmos' height,
Yet there be "lips that should be kissed,"
    Then come to-night, then come to-night.

O moon of March! so proud, so cold,
    If thus thou heedest not my prayer,
I dare to brand thee as a bold,
    Night-walking wanton of the air;—
        O vain March moon!
Henceforth, I hate thy frozen glare,
    Thy loveless and illusive light,
And so I plead in my despair,
    Come not to-night, come not to-night.

A DREAM.

I.

"Have you forgotten me?" she said,
As I, her old-time worshiper,
Stood blanched and bloodless as the dead,
And gazed upon the face of her.
  As soon may yon poor bird (thought I)
  Left mangled by the hedge to die,
  Forget the shaft that festers yet
  Within its breast,—as I forget.

II.

But, oh! each old remembered wrong
Died, in an instant, when I traced
The lines of agony that laced
The face of her I loved so long.
  I read, within her channelled cheek,
  A wretchedness no tongue could speak,—
  And so, bent with the pain of years,
  I wept,—and kissed her thro' my tears.

A SEA-WEED.

A seaman's bride knelt low beside the sea,
Her hands uplifted in dumb agony.

The rack drave in against the ragged coast,
And on the downs the raging ocean tossed.

"Give back," she cried, "O heaven, give back
    to me,
One ship, of all the ships that sail the sea."

A hurrying sea-gull, and a hungry shark
Made answer,—and the dark grew doubly
    dark.

That night, a sailor pale with outstretched
    hand,
Knelt on the deck and prayed for grace to land.

"Almighty God! let me but clasp once more,
Ere death, my waiting one, on yonder shore,"

He said,—and fell upon the shattered deck,
A lifeless mass amidst a hopeless wreck.

The boiling waters murmured a reply,
As the last bolt came rushing down the sky.

And o'er the sunken ship the sea-gulls flew,
And on the crags the night-winds blew and
    blew.

THERE IS NO LUCK ABOUT THE HOUSE.

No more the swallows dart and dip
    About my cottage-eaves; no more
The tops of my catalpas drip
    With bird-songs, as in days of yore;
My grapes are mildewed on the vine,
    My apples blighted on the boughs,
A curse has come to me and mine,
    There is no luck about the house.

The grass has withered from my lawn,
    And blasted are my chestnut trees,
From whose green domes in days agone,
    The dawn-birds poured their melodies;
The stream that vanished down the vale,
    With cups of comfort for my cows,
Has failed, at last, as all things fail—
    There is no luck about the house.

My garden now can scarce be seen,
    Gone are its beds and winding walks,
And caterpillars, lank and lean,
    Climb down the sapless hollyhocks;

My meadows of their flocks are shorn,
    The hay is moldering in my mows,
And death-worms wander in my corn—
    There is no luck about the house.

My horses and my hounds are gone,
    Nor any household pet remains,—
An owl hoots on the chimney lone,
    And bats whirl darkling thro' the panes;
Only a cricket's dreary moan,
    Or dreamy nibbling of a mouse,
Reminds me of the summers flown,—
    There is no luck about the house.

At midnight when the autumn rains
    Are chill upon the dismal flats,
I hear a sound, like clanking chains,
    Upstairs among the garret rats;
And then the ghosts of other times
    Reel round me in a mad carouse,
With all their follies and their crimes,—
    There is no luck about the house.

GENIUS.

Not those alone, who, lapped in eider down,
   And shrined in templed cities, can lay claim
To Nature's purple—to the poet's crown,
   And the proud prestige of the minstrel's fame;
Genius is even-handed! the rapt Dame
Alike salutes the beggar and the king,
   With her warm touches and her lips of flame;
Bids potentates be mute and peasants sing,
And o'er the lowliest roof outspreads her dewy wing.

With her desires ye may dispute in vain,
   Ye pampered sons of pleasure,—ye will find,
Where least expected, her supreme disdain,
   For she is fickle, and her ways are blind;
   Think not to woo her with a thoughtless mind,
Nor win her with the witcheries of art,—
   Beneath the tatters of the trampled hind,
She's quite as apt to lodge the envious dart,
As 'neath the royal robe that hides an empty heart.

A NOCTURNE.

All things that we can hear or see,
To-night, seem happy. Every tree
   Is palpitant with voice and wing,
   And vibrant with the breathing spring.
The very grass is tremulous
With music, floating up to us,
   So softly, spiritu'lly clear,
   We seem to *feel* it—not to hear.

The moonlight's luster leaking through
The bending blossoms, pearled with dew,
   Is so delicious, so divine,
   We quaff its splendor like a wine.
Only the faintest wind is curled
About the pale, enamored world,
   And drowsy perfumes slip and drip
   From every pansy's pouting lip.

Starlight, and melody and dreams!
The lover's and the poet's themes,—
   The same that once entranced and won
   The listening maids of Babylon—

A NOCTURNE.

That charm'd the ear, and caught the smiles
Of Beauty in the Grecian Isles,—
   That lulled in old Italian dells
   The Roman lads and damosels.

On such enchanting nights as these,
Our spirits, for a moment, seize
   The ravishment of life that runs,
   Exuberant, thro' stars and suns;
And as we catch the whirl and whir,
The planetary pulse and stir,
   We break the seals of sense, and scan
   The majesty of God and man.

MY GUEST.

There is a guest that I detest, forever at my side,
Who clings to me as fondly as a bridegroom to his bride;
Who leers at me, and jeers at me, and when I cross his will,
Who only smiles sardonic'ly, and hugs me closer still;
I hate him, and berate him, yet he trudges at my heels,
And reaches in my pockets, and revels at my meals;
I defy him, and would fly him, but he only presses closer,
And whispers to each wish of mine an everlasting, "No, sir."
I have chided and derided, till I'm almost out of heart,
I've abused him, and misused him, but he never will depart;—
He squeezes me, and freezes me, and well-nigh drives me mad,

He tortures and he teases me, and growls when I am glad;
He glares at me, and stares at me, as any ghoul might do,
He has shattered every promise that my soul was anchored to;
He has wrecked me, and bedecked me with the tattered garbs of woe,
He has crossed my happy threshold, and has laid my loved ones low;
He's as wary as a beagle, and he grins in such a style,
That the cunning of a serpent is apparent in his smile;
He is lank, he is lean, and his fingers are unclean,
He is ragged, he is haggard, he is spiteful and he's mean;
Than Adam he is older, than Satan he is bolder,
He's as ghastly as a skeleton, and uglier and colder;
When the winter-winds are dire, he sits crouching at my fire,
And glowering at my beggary with eyes that never tire;

He's the parent of all crime, in each country, and each clime,
And has tramped the wide world over, hand in hand, with Father Time;
His record all may read, in the hearts that break and bleed,
On the lips of little children that forever pine and plead;
And his deeds are further written, over sleepless eyes red-litten,
Over cold and empty cradles, over roofs by sorrow smitten;
Over shattered hopes once cherished, over pleasures that have perished,
Over broken dreams of glory, that a better manhood nourished;
In the byways, and the highways, he goes onward unmolested,
And wakes the world to labor ere its weary hands are rested;
He's a beggar, and a ranger, and was present, not a stranger,
At the birth of the Messiah, in the cold Judean manger;
He has trailed along the path of the tempest in its wrath,

And has gloated o'er the ruins of the mouldered aftermath;
He's the Prince of Empty Pockets, out at elbow and at knee,
He's a knight without a copper, whom we nickname—*Poverty*.

A VISION.

And in my dream of beauty, I beheld
    A being rapt and radiant as a star,
Beneath whose kindling light my spirit swelled
    To melody—and, streaming from afar,
I saw the specters of the dawn unbar
    The gates of morning; and on every gale,
That blew around Aurora's bannered car,
I saw the Summer's censer-swingers trail
    Their odorous incense over hill and dale.

And on my sight uprose a golden mist,
    Peopled with many a floating form and fair,—
A Paradise of wandering souls, I wist,
    Chained to the shifting Eden of the air,
In snowy cavalcades of sweet despair;
    And some had harps and sang, and some had flowers,
And others crowns,—and all were *debonair*;
    And everywhere were grottos, glades, and bowers,
    And purling fountains, vistas, shrines, and towers.

THE FIRST GRAY HAIR.

And thou hast come at last,
Thou baleful issue of the buried years—
Sad fruitage of the past,—
Root-nurtured in a loam of hopes and fears;
I hail thee, but I hate thee, lurking there,
Thou first gray hair.

Thou soft and silken coil,
Thou milk-white blossom in a midnight
tress!
Out from the alien soil,
I'll pluck thee in thine infant tenderness,
As the rude husbandman uproots the tare,
Thou first gray hair.

Of all the fleecy flock,
Thou art the one to loathe and to despise;
The cheat within the shock,
The mould that on the early harvest lies,
The mildew on the blossoms of the pear—
Thou first gray hair.

And thou the Judas art,
The tattler of old Time, who doth betray
The weary worn-out heart,
Ere yet we dare to dream of its decay;
Thou art a hint of wreck beyond repair,
Thou first gray hair.

EDISON.

Upon a time at Menlo Park,
   A merry genius wrought,
Day after day, from dawn to dark,
   The cunning webs of thought;
And as his nimble fancy drew
   The threads of doubt apart,
Strange fabrics 'neath his fingers grew,
   To wondrous forms of art.

To words articulate he gave
   The wings of wider flight;
He made the human voice his slave,
   And robbed the earth of night;
Of speech he caught the subtle sound,
   And treasured it so clear,
That dead men, lying underground,
   May still be talking here.

The wizards of the elder age
   Have dwindled into naught,
Beside this later heritage,
   This Heracles of thought

With spider-energy he weaves
    The gossamers that bind,
Through every land, in richer sheaves,
    The hearts of all mankind.

THE VALE OF GOLD.

(They tell of a wonderful valley in the Sierra Madre, which glistens with gold and is resplendent with bright waters and beautiful flowers. Connected with it are many fascinating legends of Indian origin, the prettiest of which is the belief of the natives that Montezuma will some day return and free them from the dominion of the descendants of the Conquestodores.)

Far to the south and west there lies,
   Away in the sun-set land,
Where the weird Sierra lifts to the skies
   The wealth of her jeweled hand—
There lies deep hid in the mountain range,
   As old as the world is old,
A fabulous valley, dim and strange,
   That is known as the Vale of Gold.

Never a white man's foot has crossed
   An Eden as fair as this,
Since bidding adieu to the one he lost,
   On the brim of the world, I wis;
There are flowers as bright as the orbs of night,
   And birds of radiant wing—
And streams that quiver and dance forever,
   In time to the tunes they sing.

There's a golden grot, and a golden ledge,
    And blooms of gold, and golden bees,—
Gold in the grass, and the sighing sedge,
    And gold in the orange trees;
There's gold in the stars, and gold in the stream,
    And gold in the skin of the snake—
Gold in the moon when the dreamers dream,
    And gold in the morn, when they wake.

And a seer hath writ on a golden stone,
    In a golden time of the past,
How the Montezumas will mount their throne
    Again in the valley vast;
And the fires of the Aztec priests will burn
    Once more on the altars cold,
And the gods of the vanquished race return,
    To reign in the Vale of Gold.

THE CRIME.

Here lived the slayer, and there the slain,
　With barely an acre of ground between;
'Twas night! they stood in the wind and rain,
And quarrelled,—next morning a ghastly stain
　Of blood on the meadow-grass was seen.

And one was dead, and one had fled,
　And all night long the mourners wept;
The widow wailed in the dusk by the dead,
And the wife of the slayer shook with dread,
　And the north-wind over the chimney swept.

And these were farmers, and these were friends,
　Friends, I say, till that night in the Fall;
Too proud was the one to make amends
For a foolish wrong, and the bloody ends
　Of passion followed, with grief and gall.

Then a gibbet loomed in the dusky sky,
　And a blue-eyed orphan pierced the night
With desolate sobs, and a móther's cry
Outrang the blast, as it whistled by,
　In its wild, unbridled flight.

They laid the slayer not far from the slain,
    In the village church-yard, under the hill,
And the meadows of death were dearth of
    grain,
And the winds blew over the unplowed plain,
    For the hands of the husbandmen were still.

I passed by the crumbling huts, to-day,
    And birds were out, and the land was green;
Two women withered, and bent, and gray,
Sat, each in the shade of her own doorway,
    And children played on the ground between.

MARCH.

The gables of the farm-house groan,
    And down the orchard's barren rows,
    Beyond the hills, a cloud of crows
Against the windy west is blown.

The falling sun is fringed with mist,
    And east-ward like an Indian queen,
    The moon at intervals is seen,
Thro' dripping rifts of amethyst.

A few stray flakes of snow—and then,
    The all-night pattering on the pane
    Of slumber-wooing sleet and rain—
Then morning—and the winds again!

SHE SLEEPS.

'Twas summer's noon! One I had known
    Lay stark upon her lily bed;
And one I knew not, wept alone,
    Beside the lady lying dead;—
The lady with the long brown hair,
    And lucent eyes of Heaven's own blue,—
A lady fair and *debonaire*,
    As e'er was given man to woo.

He wept for eyes that ne'er again
    Would lift their love-light to his own—
His tears fell like the autumn rain,
    O'er days of joy forever flown;
He wept as one might weep who stands
    Outside the pale of Paradise,
When some sweet saint with pleading hands
    Floats, dream-like, o'er his tranced eyes.

He wept the tender heart and true,
    That fell to dust before his eye—
He wept as knightly spirits do,
    O'er all the beauty that can die;

He wept to hear his orphans cry,
 Amid the gloom, the long night through,—
He wept until his soul was dry
 Then slept—and woke to weep anew.

And in and out the people drew,
 And much they marveled—much they praised
The lady's loveliness, whereto
 Death's awful signet had been placed;
And kinsmen from the fair land round
 Came in with weeping lids and lips,
And round the marble mother bound
 Their garlands,—love's Apocalypse!

She's gone into the silent land,
 She's faded from this world of ours,—
Where summer's golden skies expand,
 She's folded in a realm of flowers;
She sleeps—the fair young mother sleeps,—
 No words of ours, no cries, no tears,
Can pierce the dull grave's gloomy deeps,
 Thro' all the intervital years.

She sleeps,—nor any dreams hath she,—
 The tides may ebb, the tides may flow;

Where once she was, she ne'er can be,
   While round the world the wild winds
      blow;
She sleeps—God rest her where she lies!
   Until the gates of dawn unbar,
Then give her spirit strength to rise
   To life in some sublimer star!

'WAY DOWN IN SPICE VALLEY.

I.

'Way down in Spice Valley I'm drifting
    to-night,
On a river of dreams, with a heart that is light
As the lilt of the woodlark, a-tilt on the tree,
By the spot where my cot in that vale used
    to be—
When life was a lily just opening its eye,
To the dew of the dawn, and the blue of
    the sky,
    'Way down in Spice Valley.

II.

'Way down in Spice Valley, in fancy, I see
The bloom of the clover still beck'ning the bee—
The low-leaning orchards, the herds on the hill,
And the road, like a ribbon unspooled, to the
    mill;
Still, still, in my dream, I can see the old
    stream,

And the ford, where the farmer drove over his team,
>'Way down in Spice Valley.

III.

'Way down in Spice Valley, Old Time falls asleep,
With his head on the sward, in a slumber so deep
That the birds cannot wake him, with melodies blithe,
And the long valley-grasses grow over his scythe,—
And Summer kneels down, in her long golden gown,
On a carpet of green, where the skies never frown,
>'Way down in Spice Valley.

IV.

'Way down in Spice Valley, my memory goes,
With a sigh, like the sob of the river that flows
In that far-away vale,—and I pray in my dream,

To be borne, when I die, to that beautiful
    stream,
And tenderly laid in the welcoming shade
Of the wide-spreading woods, where I wandered
    and played,
       'Way down in Spice Valley.

A FRAGMENT.

There is no panacea known
To soothe the soul when hope is flown—
There is no balm the wound to heal,
When Love withdraws his dripping steel.

The mangled heart may still beat on,
When everything it prized is gone—
Throb on, without one pleasing pain,
To indicate if life remain.

God pity him who cannot die,
When all his dreams in ashes lie,
And through his soul's dismantled hall
The spectral past holds carnival.

THE OLD HOUSE-FLY.

I.

Go throw the shutters open wide, and lift the windows high,
Let out the silence and the gloom, let in the jolly fly;
I'm weary of this stale repose, and long to hear again,
The sweetest sound of all the year, the fly upon the pane;--
I long to see him bobbing up and down the sill and sash,
I long to feel his tickling tread upon my soft mustache;
I love to see him tilting on his slender, tender toes,
I love to watch him bump, and buzz, and balance on his nose;
In all the universe, to-day, of merry song and glee,
O, tell me where's another that is happier than he;

Then throw the shutters open wide, and lift
   the windows high,
Let out the gloom and silence, and let in the
   jolly fly.

II.

O, the old house-fly! O, the brave house-fly!
A straddling o'er the butter-dish, a sprawling
   o'er the pie,—
A jogging thro' the jell and jam, and jouncing
   round the cream,
As prone to risk a summer sail upon the milky
   stream;
A roving life the rascal leads thro' all the rosy
   hours,
A sipping only of the sweets, and skipping all
   the sours;
A button-headed roustabout, a lover light and
   bold,
Who revels on the ripest lips that mortal eyes
   behold;
Who clambers up the softest cheek, and up
   the whitest arm,
And loiters on the fairest breast that ever love
   made warm;

Then throw the shutters open wide, and lift
  the windows high,
Let out the silence and the gloom, let in the
  jolly fly.

III.

O, the old house-fly! O, the jolly house-fly!
He was present at our coming, he'll be with
  us when we die;
From Turkestan to Mexico, his broad dominion
  runs,
And his nature never changes with the
  "process of the suns;"
From the days of dusky Cheops, down thro'
  centuries of dirt,
'Tis a matter of conjecture, if he ever washed
  his shirt;
He has dined with every poet from the
  patriarchal Chaucer,
He has often taken pleasure-trips in Billy
  Shakespeare's saucer;
He dipped his saucy noddle into Cleopatra's
  cup,
When the amorous Antonius his kingdom
  offered up;

Then throw the shutters open wide, and lift the windows high,
Let out the silence and the gloom, let in the jolly fly.

IV

O, the old house-fly! O, the naughty house-fly!
He dances on the baby's lip, and on the dead man's eye;
He's first to taste the tawny wine within the tippler's glass,
He prances on the prelate's nose whene'er he goes to mass;
He's found within the skipper's hut, and in the gilded hall,
A giddy gambolier, who pays his compliments to all;
When our mothers rocked the cradles, in the cabins of our birth,
His happy chorus blended with the cricket on the hearth,—
And I love the recollection of the hours I've seen him crawl,

In the summer-time of childhood, up and down
    the whitened wall;
Then throw the shutters open wide, and lift
    the windows high,
Let out the gloom and silence, and let in the
    jolly fly.

INSOMNIA.

I

Into the dark and chambered deep,
   I wearily cast my eye,
And cry to the echoing night for sleep,
   But ever in vain I cry.

II

For the wheels of memory turn,
   And passions old arise,
And the wasted years come back and burn
   The slumber out of my eyes.

III

And I sob like a child in pain,
   For the rest that comes not nigh,
And out in the dark I hear the rain,
   Where my shattered idols lie.

"THEY HAD NO POET AND SO THEY DIED."

In the dim waste lands of the Orient stands
    The wreck of a race so old and vast,
That the grayest legend can not lay hands
    On a single fact of its tongueless past;
Not even the red gold crown of a king,
    Nor a warrior's shield, nor aught beside,
Can history out of the ruins wring,—
    They had no poet and so they died.

Babel and Nineveh, what are they,
    But feeble hints of a passing power
That over the populous East held sway,
    In a dream of pomp for a paltry hour?
A toppled tower, and a shattered stone,
    Where the satyrs dance, and the dragons hide,
Is all that is known of the glory flown,—
    They had no poet and so they died.

Down where the dolorous Congo slips,
    Like a tawny snake, thro' the torrid clime,

Man's soul has slept in a cold eclipse,
　　On the world's dark rim, since the dawn of
　　　　time;
And if ever the ancient Nubians wrought
　　A work of beauty, or strength, or pride,
It was unrecorded, and goes for naught,—
　　They had no poet and so they died.

And even here, in the sun-crowned West,
　　In the land we love, in the vales we've trod,
Where the bleeding palms of the world find
　　　　rest
　　On Freedom's lap, at the feet of God,—
Even here, I say, ere the earth waxed old,
　　A race Titanic did once abide,
But, ah! their story is left untold,—
　　They had no poet and so they died.

The same old tale! and so it will be,
　　As long as the heavens feed the stars,—
As long as the tribes of men shall see
　　A lesser glory in arts than wars;
And so let us live, and labor, and pray,
　　As down we glide with the darkling tide,
That never a singer of us may say,
　　They had no poet and so they died.

AT WATERLOO.

"Stand firm!" said the Duke, as a courier came
Thro' the battery's breath, with his bare brow aflame;
"Stand firm!"—"But we perish"—"Stand firm!" cried the Duke,
And the officer flushed as he felt the rebuke,
But he coolly replied, 'mid the roar of the gun,
"You'll find us all here when the battle is done."

Death's carnival followed. O'er field and o'er trench,
In billows of doom, dashed the waves of the French;
As firm as a sea-battered wall stood the rank
Of that fated brigade,—not an English heart shrank,—
Together they perished, but Wellington won,
He found them all there when the battle was done.

"GAUN HAME."

"Fareweel!" she said, and she waved her hand
From the stately ship, as it left the land
For a far-off shore.
        "Fareweel!" said she,
"I am gaun awa' to my ain countree,
Where the gowans grow, and my laddie lies
Cauld in his grave, where the Ochils rise,—
To the land o' the leal, where my mither dear,
Has slumbered for mony a lang, lang year.
Ghaist-like, I've wandered the warld sae wide,
A wae-worn lassie—an unlo'ed bride,—
An' now, as the simmer grows sad and sere,
An' my days draw doun to the last dim year,
I am driftin' awa' frae a frien'less shore,
To the hame o' the happy, ance more, ance more."

   *   *   *   *   *   *   *

The ship went down in the roaring sea,
But the lady—she reached her "ain countree."

A BALLAD OF TEARS.

I

"The tears I shed must ever fall,"
   Low moaned a mother, as she kept
A nightly vigil over all
   Her household idols, as they slept;
The storm came down against the pane,
   She heard, far off, strange voices call,
As still she sobbed, in drear refrain,
   "The tears I shed must ever fall."

II

"The tears I shed must ever fall,"
   Sighed one—an aged man— who stood
Beside a tablet, gray and tall,
   Far in a churchyard's solitude;
The past burned back upon his brain,
   With dreams of bliss beyond recall,—
Poor soul! he whispered thro' his pain,
   "The tears I shed must ever fall."

III

"The tears I shed must ever fall,"
    A hungry, houseless exile wailed,
As o'er him, from a festal-hall,
    The lights of joy and splendor trailed.
He wept,—his weeping was in vain,
    For death itself could not forestall
The anguish of his cold refrain,
    "The tears I shed must ever fall."

IV

"The tears I shed must ever fall,"
    A lone girl sang, and singing, heard
The waves beat on the dim sea-wall,
    In mournful melody and weird;
The night caught up the plaintive strain,
    As, folding round her, like a pall,
It rustled to the dull refrain,
    "The tears I shed must ever fall."

JULY IN THE WEST.

DAY.

A rhythm of reapers; a flashing
Of steels in the meadows; a lashing
Of sheaves in the wheatlands; a glitter
Of grain-builded streets, and a twitter
   Of birds in a motionless sky,—
      And that is July!

A rustle of corn-leaves; a tinkle
Of bells on the hills; a twinkle
Of sheep in the lowlands; a bevy
Of bees where the clover is heavy;
   A butterfly blundering by,—
      And that is July!

NIGHT.

A moon-flood prairie; a straying
Of light-hearted lovers; a baying
Of far-away watch dogs; a dreaming
Of brown-fisted farmers; a gleaming
   Of fire-flies eddying nigh,—
      And that is July!

A babble of brooks that deliver
Their flower-purfled waves to the river;
A moan in the marshes; in thickets,
A dolorous droning of crickets,
  Attuned to a whippoorwill's cry,—
  And that is July!

ILLINOIS.

I sing not of the summer-lands,
   That lie beyond the rolling seas—
   Nor of the famed Hesperides,
Nor any tropic isles nor strands.

I sing a land of peace and light,
   Of labor, love and liberty—
   A land wherein the prophets see
The dawn of progress infinite.

No dreaming poet ever drew
   Upon the tablet of his thought,
   A land with fairer promise fraught,
Than this that opens on my view.

The maiden empire of the West,
   Gold-sheened, gold-sandalled, and gold-crowned,
   Her brows with yellow harvests bound,
Her ample bosom blossom-drest.

Here rhythmic rivers flash and flow,
   Thro' meadows measureless, and here,

On banks of roses, cities rear
Their temples in the sunset's glow.

Here birds of every tongue and tinge
   Fly up and down the laughing lands,
   From Michigan's surf-whitened sands,
To where Ohio's floods infringe.

The skies of Italy are ours,
   And ours the Lydian airs that blow
So lightly, lullingly, and low,
   At night-tide, o'er the sleeping flowers.

No ghostly ruins fret the wind,
   No shattered shrines, no toppling towers,
   But, ah! this peaceful realm embowers
The wealth of Ormus and of Ind.

Nor is the soul of romance flown,
   For here the poet's eye can trace
   The vestige of a vanished race,
In field and forest, stream and stone.

And here a grander Rome will rise,
   A Rome without a slave or king,
   Round which a nobler race will spring,
With patriotic souls and wise;—

A free-born people, proud and great,
   With heart and hand to do and dare,—
   With strength to fashion firm and fair
The fabric of the growing State.

And Greece, beneath these western skies,
   Will leap to life again, and breathe
   Her spirit into stone, and wreathe
The land with deathless melodies.

I trow no fancy can forecast
   The fame, the splendor yet to be
   Unscrolled before the world, when we
Are drawn into the dreamless past.

"THE EYES OF ELEANORA."

I.

As the light of a star is found,
By day, in the sunless ground,
   Where the river of silence lies,—
So the spirit of beauty dwells,
O love, in the mimic wells
   Of thy large, thy luminous eyes.

II

As out of a turbulent night,
A lost bird turns to the light
   Of a desolate dreamer's room,—
So, forth from the storm of thine eyes,
A passionate splendor flies
   To my soul, through the inter-gloom.

III

As a lily quivers and gleams,
All night, by the darkling streams,
   That dream in the underlands,—
So, up from the haunted lakes
Of thy shadowy eyes, Love shakes
   The snows of her beck'ning hands.

IV

As clusters of new worlds dawn,
When the infinite night comes on,
   In the measureless, moonless skies—
So the planet of love burns high,
O sweet, when the day sweeps by,
   In the dusk of thy orient eyes.

O, BLEAK IS THE NIGHT.
(*Song.*)

O bleak is the night
   That is shorn of its stars,
And cold is the heart
   That is chastened with scars;
But bleaker and colder
   Than everything yet,
Is the love-plundered bosom,
   That cannot forget.

The bright crystal dews
   That o'er-sprinkle the lawn,
Slip back into mist
   At the touch of the dawn,—
But the lover low-chained
   To the rack of regret,
Must languish in pain,
   For he cannot forget.

White sails of the ocean
   Grow dingy on shore,
But brighten again
   As they sweep the seas o'er;

Not so the fond eyes
   With love's hopelessness wet—
The heart never lightens
   That cannot forget.

The visions of terror
   That haunt us by night,
Like shadows take wing
   At the first flush of light;
But the breast of despair
   Still in anguish must fret,
For the curse is upon it—
   It cannot forget.

THE BURDEN OF BABYLON.

O Babylon, O Babylon,
  The Lord hath made His purpose known;
His anger, like a seething sea,
    Swells at thy gate,
    And Sodom's fate
Alas, proud city, is reserved for thee.

O Babylon, O Babylon,
  Soon, soon, thy glory shall be gone;
Beneath thy godless roofs shall run
    E'en the warm blood
    Of motherhood,   [one!
And none escape His vengeance—nay, not

O Babylon, O Babylon,
  Never again as years go on,
Shall shepherds fold their flocks by thee;
    Nor Arab pitch
    His tent, nor hitch
His camel by thy cool pomegranate tree.

O Babylon, O Babylon,
  The winds shall o'er thy ruins moan;
Within thy desolated halls,
    Shall flit the owl,
    And wild beasts prowl,
And dancing satyrs hold their carnivals.

BEHIND THE VEIL.

I

As a painter walked forth in the dawn, half-adream,
    He saw the green splendor of sumptuous trees
Waving under the winds, and his eyes drank the gleam
    Of the blue vagues above him like pendulous seas;
The world was a picture, so fair and so fine,
    That the artist beheld it with marvelling eyes,—
But he saw not the hand of the Painter divine,
    Who stood at his easel, just back of the skies.

II

A sculptor once strolled mid' the mountains, entranced,
    Untongued, in a tremulous transport of Art,

As he scanned the grim turrets of granite that
    glanced
  On the rim of the sun, standing stark and
    apart;
His soul sipped the scene till it reeled with
    despair,
  Till his chisel fell dulled on the stones at
    his feet,—
But he saw not the Sculptor, half-hid on the
    stair,
  And he heard not the mallet of God as it
    beat.

III

In fancy, I saw a musician enchained
  In a tangle of melodies, tremblingly twirled
From the throats of the throstles, like sym-
    phonies strained
  From the harps of old minstrels, and blown
    down the world;
He stood in the dawning, delirously dazed,
  And as still as a bronze,—but he saw not all,
The swinging batoon that the Master upraised
  At the Fount of all music, just over the wall.

IV

I saw, in my vision, a poet who wrote
    With a pencil of light, from a heart that was fraught
With the fervor of passion,—whose soul was afloat
    On a palpitant ocean of fancy and thought;
His lays by the lips of all lands were rehearsed,
    Till they set the slow pulse of the peoples a-quiver,—
But he saw not the face of the Poet, who first
    Gave the song to the sea, and the rhyme to the river.

DAY AND NIGHT.

I

When drowsy Day draws round his downy
    bed
The Tyrian tapestries of gold and red,
    And, weary of his flight,
    Puts out the palace light,—
      'Tis night!

II

When languid Night, awakening with a yawn,
Leaps down the moon-washed stairway of the
    dawn,
    In trailing disarray,
    Sweeping the dews away,—
      'Tis day!

ONE GOLDEN HAIR.

(*Found in an old volume of Burns.*)

A woman's hair! a single strand!
   And yet a most fantastic thought
   Flashed o'er me, as my fingers caught
And drew it forth across my hand.

Like to some living thing that turns,
   Instinctive, from the spoiler's touch,
   The hair curled upward from my clutch,
And sought again the page of Burns,—
A page whereon the bard had told
   A woman's charms, in verse divine:—
" Her hair was like the links o' gold,
   Her cheeks like lilies dipped in wine."

A woman's hair! a single shred!
   A golden fibre gently torn
   From some proud beauty to adorn
The book of love, wherein she read,—
Wherein she caught the flash and fire
   Of purest passion ever given,
To sanctify a poet's lyre,
   And lure a panting heart to heaven.

A golden hair! a slender thing!
  A soft and silken coil! And yet,
  In death, it still would pay a debt
Of love unto the poet-king.
This single hair—this twining hair,
  A sweeter, nobler tribute pays
To him who sang beside the Ayr,
  Than any human lip can phrase.

IN SUMMER WOODS.

How sweet amidst the melancholy hills
To lie, a lazy dreamer, in the lap
Of flush mid-summer, drowsy with the lull
Of lapping waters and light winds that pipe
In murmurous monotones, along the dim,
Sun-litten arcades of the spectral woods,—
To hear, remotely, in the lonesome lands,
The drony resonance of dreamy bells,
Where, 'mid cool shadows, lurk the browsing
 herds,
In dimpled hollows, soft with summer sward—
To list the sullen rasp of insect wings,
And, in a silken indolence of soul,
To note the bluster of the tippling bee,
Home-reeling from the pillaged palaces
Of Flora's shining empire.
           Every tuft
Is populous with panting life and toil—
Each tree is tremulous with melody,
Each dainty leaf, each dewy blade of grass,
Stirs into music at the gentlest touch
Of every passing wind.
           Ye who would hear
The primal symphonies by Adam heard,

Amid the velvet vales of Paradise,
Go down, go down, to the embowering woods,
Go down into the pulsing, summer woods,
Forgetful and forgotten of the world,
And in a rosy rhapsody of rest,
Throw wide the spirit's portals to the fresh,
Out-flowing voices of the universe,—
The voices of the everlasting hills,
The voices of the rivers and the rocks,
The rivulets, the rushes, and the reeds,
And all the wizard-rhythm of the shades.

Let the light spirit, loosened from the thrall
Of every-day distraction, wander free,
And quaff the nectar of a nobler hope,
The sweeter incense of a higher sphere,
And, on the star-crowned summits of the mind,
Model ambitions of sublimer mould.

SEVERED FRIENDSHIP.

Shall we never meet again?
Is it fated that we twain
   Shall know no more the clasping
   Of each other's arms—the grasping
Of each other's hands, and tingling
Of the old-time's intermingling?

Is it written—is it known,
In the doom-book at the Throne,
   That you and I, forever,
   Shall never, never, never,
Be united—be twin-hearted,
As in days long since departed?

May we never backward creep,
Thro' the shadows, vague and deep,
   To the melancholy borders
   Of our strifes and our disorders,
And restore the fetters golden
Of the happy days and olden?

Is it fated that we twain
Must forevermore remain
   Asunder, but still yearning
   For a love that's unreturning—
For a friendship rashly riven,
In the sight of Earth and Heaven?

MY LADY BEAUTIFUL.

Could I, in two sweet sonnets, here condense
   The honied praise and compliments of all
   The poets of the earth since Adam's fall,—
Or could my light-winged fancy, flying thence,
Beyond the girdling barricades of sense,
   The subtle strength of future song forestall—
   Were such my gifts, I'd build a temple tall
Of royal homage, walled with eloquence,
Within whose purple court, upon a throne
   Of silken despotism, I would place
The snowy empress of my soul's desire;—
Her dynasty should be my heart, alone,
   Her passions be to mine as food and fire,
And pasture for mine eyes her body's grace.

And twinkling Cupids nightly to her sleep,
   In clouds of riant rivalry would throng,—
   And in the meshes of her ringlets long,
A breathless vigil o'er the dreamer keep;
Nor ever should a tell-tale teardrop peep
   From out her dewy lids,—nor from her tongue
   Should aught escape but laughter and sweet song,

And discourse dreamfully devout and deep.
No pirate winds—no prowling plagues should creep,
  By night or day, within her wreathen shrine,—
The stairway to her heart should be so steep,
  That it would echo to no tread but mine,—
And I, through all the dear Idalian days,
Would lull the princess with love's roundelays.

IN SOUDAN.

Ended that strange career,
    Long so victorious,
Slain by an Arab's spear,
    Gordon, the glorious;
Stark under torrid skies,
    Girdled with gloom,
Britain's best soldier lies
    Dead in Khartoum.

Stewart falls bleeding, and
    Earle is in glory,—
Steady, now! hand to hand,
    Sweep all before ye!
Close up the shattered square,
    Stand fast, who can!
Strike! while a hope is there
    Left in Soudan.

Mothers of England, weep!
    Weep, sons and daughters!
Weep for the brave who sleep,
    Hard by Nile's waters!
Weep for your Burnaby
    Dead in the van,—
Weep ye, for all who lie
    Cold in Soudan.

OUT ON THE FARM.

A home in the country! what care I
    For the tossing town, with its madd'ning din,
Where the grinding wheels of the world go by,
    And the soul grows sick, as the crowds crush in;
Better the lanes where the linnets be,
    And the brown bees drone in the dewy thyme;
Where the wild bird flutes on the tulip-tree,
    And the garnet bells of the pawpaws chime.

A home in the country! Never for me
    The flash of fashion, and feverish beat
Of the trampling masses my sad eyes see
    Pulsing forever from street to street;—
Better the woods where the waters meet,
    And the grass grows cool by the shelvy shore,—
Where the wild-flowers blush in their dim retreat,
And the clamor of town is heard no more.

A home in the country, blessed and sweet,
    From the hand of God, where the shade and shine

Play all day long in the rippling wheat,
    And the berries glow in the grass, like wine;
Never a home in the town be mine,
    Mid' the stir and whir, and the gaud and glare,—
Give me the farm where the clovered kine
    Are heard on the hill,—and the world is fair.

THE OLD FIREPLACE.

The blessed old fireplace! how bright it appears,
    As back to my boyhood I gaze,
O'er the desolate waste of the vanishing years,
    From the gloom of these lone latter-days;
Its lips are as ruddy, its heart is as warm
    To my fancy, to-night, as of yore,
When we cuddled around it, and smiled at the storm,
    As it showed its white teeth at the door.

I remember the apple that wooed the red flame,
    Till the blood bubbled out of its cheek,—
And the passionate popcorn that smothered its shame,
    Till its heart split apart with a shriek;
I remember the Greeks and the Trojans who fought,
    In their shadowy shapes on the wall,
And the yarn, in thick tangles, my fingers held taut
    While my mother was winding the ball.

I remember the cat that lay cozy and curled
    By the jamb, where the flame flickered high,

And the sparkles,—the fire-flies of winter,—
    that whirled
      Up the flue, as the wind whistled by;
I remember the bald-headed, bandy-legg'd
    tongs,
      That frowned like a fiend in my face,
In a fury of passion, repeating the wrongs
      They had borne in the old fireplace.

I remember the steam from the kettle that
    breathed,
      As soft as the flight of a soul,—
The long-handled skillet that spluttered and
    seethed
      With the batter that burthened its bowl;
I remember the rusty, identical nail,
      Where the criminal pot-hooks were hung,—
The dragon-faced andirons, the old cedar pail,
      The gourd, and the peg where it swung.

But the fire has died out on the old cabin
    hearth,
      The wind clatters loud thro' the pane,
And the dwellers,—they're flown to the ends
    of the earth,
      And will gaze on it never again;

A forget-me-not grows in the mouldering wall,
    The last as it were of its race,
And the shadows of night settle down like a pall,
    On the stones of the old fireplace.

"JOUKYDADDLES."

O, where is Joukydaddles,
   O, where, where, where—
The little chubby codger
   That was toddlin' here and there,
With the jelly on his chin,
   And the butter on his cheeks,
And his lubber little legs
   With their puddle-muck streaks?

O, where is Joukydaddles,
   O, where, where, where—
With the bonnie breezes blowin'
   In his curly brown hair;
The little busy-body
   In his berry-stained shirt,
A-dabblin' with his wee,
   Tawny fingers in the dirt?

O, where is Joukydaddles,
   O, where, where, where—
Who daily used to tumble
   Down the old cellar-stair;

The burly little bandit,
  With the big jewelled eyes,—
The bloody buccaneer
  'Mong the bugs and butterflies?

O, where is Joukydaddles,
  O, where, where, where,—
We never see him here,
  And we never hear him there;
There's a shadow at the threshold,
  A silence on the floor,
And a dusty little roundabout
  Is danglin' on the door;
We call—but Joukydaddles
  Never answers any more.

LINES TO A TERRAPIN.

O, terrapin, terrapin, whither away,
   Thou slow-moving, evil-eyed tramp;
What destiny tempts thee, old pilgrim, to stray
   So far from the terrapin camp?
Why prowl at my garden, thou sauntering crust
   Of inscrutable cunning,—why sneak
And recoil, like a snake, with an air of distrust,
   When a gentleman deigneth to speak?

Thou toothless, old triple-lashed rover, what news
   Bringest thou from the terrapin isles,—
And what of thy trip thro' the dusks and the dews,
   O'er the pathless and perilous miles?
What bloody banditti beleaguer thy way,
   And where does thy lone journey trend,—
O, prince of the turtles, make answer, I pray,
   To the querulous poet, thy friend!

Thou Wandering Jew of the terrapin race,
    What marvelous mysteries lie
Tormentingly locked in thy taciturn face,
    And forever unsealed in thine eye;
For thee doth some terrapin mistress await
    In her portable palace, I wot,—
For thee sits she night after night at the gate,
    And sadly complains of her lot.

O, terrapin, terrapin, whither away,
    Thro' the dews and the dazzle of dawn?
No longer, poor gypsy, thy steps I will stay,
    But will think of thee often, when gone;
Thy road is as rugged no doubt as my own,
    Thy heart is as sunless and sore,—
So I wish thee good-morning, thou terrapin lone,
    And bid thee godspeed from my door.

A PROFILE OF FALL.

Under the tree the ladder leans
   On the branches gray and old,—
And, balanced above, the gleaner gleans
   The glittering spheres of gold;
While pyramids brighter than maiden's eyes,
In the leafy aisles of the orchard rise.

Rambo, Pippin, and Limbertwig,
   Belleflower, Russet, and Romanite,
Dangling high on the slender sprig,
   Gleam with a quivering rainbow light,—
And the old man nodding beneath the trees,
Dreams of the times when he planted these.

When a blue-eyed bride was at his side,
   In the merry summer weather,
And life was fair as the apples there,
   That cling to the bough together;—
But a score of springs have showered their bloom
Where the sunlight lies on the good wife's tomb.

With a greedy mouth the cider-mill
    Is craunching away in the grove,—
Its lips adrip with an amber rill
    As pure as the wine of Jove;
And the bees and the nut-brown boys are there,
To sip the sweets and the sport to share.

The chestnut brown in a sheath of spears
    On the fading hillside lies,
And sleeps till the sunlight bursts its burrs
    And shakes the night from its eyes;
And the walnut cloaked in Lincoln-green,
Dreams of a winter night, I ween.

Up in the old oak's airy hall,
    The squirrel heaps his store,
In spite of the deadly rifle-ball
    That rings at his chamber door,—
A merry fellow and full of glee,
Is the fur-clad knight of the hollow tree.

All day long in his lampless log,
    The lonesome rabbit lies,
Peeking at every passing dog
    With big sardonic eyes,—

And wondering to himself, no doubt,
If ever the dog will find him out.

The feathered bards have sheathed their quills,
    And closed each tuneful mouth,
And flown like sunshine out of the hills
    To summer lands of the South;
And we who sit in the shade and write,
Sigh to them all, as they wing their flight.

A VALENTINE.

Tho' hill and vale with music ring,
And mating birds be on the wing,
To-day I have no heart to sing,—
   My Margerie no longer hears,
   She smiles not now, nor heeds my tears,
She wakes not with the waking spring,
   She comes not with returning years.

As sink the snow-flakes in the sea,
Loved Margerie, lost Margerie,
My thoughts concenter all in thee;
   To-day the softest, subtlest note
   That trembles from the throstle's throat,
Stirs not the slightest pulse in me,—
   My dreams are of a day remote.

The lute lies silent on my knee,
I touch no more the trembling key,
That thrilled the heart of Margerie;
   Those eyes where truth and passion met,
   Love's planets, in the grave have set,
And left this heritage to me,
   A memory—a fond regret.

'TIS ALWAYS SUNDAY IN THE WOODS.

" 'Tis always Sunday in the woods,"
    She said—the bonnie wife of mine—
As thro' the leaf-walled solitudes,
    We passed beneath the arching vine;
We saw the sunbeams slant and shine,
    Like tongues of flame at Pentecost,—
We sipped the sacramental wine,
    From many a chalice gold-emboss'd.

Outlined against the templed hills,
    The living symbols of the Lord,
We saw,—and down a thousand rills
    The praises of His name were poured;
Above us mighty organs roared,
    And hidden pipers blew and blew
Such strains of heavenly accord,
    As never art attaineth to.

The aisles were carpeted with flowers,
    The pews with emerald were plushed,
And from a hundred wreathen towers,
    The silver chimes of morning gushed;

Anon, and all the space was hushed,
   As when, within cathedrals dim,
The body of the Christ is crushed,
   And Christians quaff the blood of Him.

'Tis always Sunday in the woods!
   The cattle down the valley pass,
In lazy-moving multitudes,
   To where the river gleams like glass;
The birds, in one symphonic mass
   Of benedictions, flood the airs,
And all the insect-haunted grass
   Is sibilant with whispered prayers.

Around the rock-built altars crowd
   The patient oaks, as prone to pour
Their pæans to the bannered cloud
   In golden glory floating o'er;
Green-robed, they stand forevermore,
   Within their dreamy vastitudes,
Devout as Druids to the core—
   'Tis always Sunday in the woods.

FOR AN ALBUM.

We shall meet, we shall greet,
    Where the bright lights quiver
Over yonder, on the heights
    Of the interflowing river,—
Over yonder where the moon
    With the shepherd-boy dallies,
And the goat-foot Pan
    Goes piping down the valleys,—
We shall meet, we shall greet,
    Where the warm sky showers
The pearls of the planets
    On the fountains and the flowers,—
Where the summer lies asleep
    On the wings of the swallows,
And the nightingale sings
    In the dream-haunted hollows;
We shall meet, over there,
    On the sunny hills seven,
In the Rome of the soul,
    In the Italy of Heaven.

WHEN YOUR FATHER WENT TO WAR.

I.

When your father went to war, Jennie, you were but a child,
A romping little rowdy, running riotous and wild
In the maple-shaded pasture, where our cottage used to stand,
And we owned a timbered forty of the richest river land,—
Yes, owned it—every inch of it—by labor's hard decree,
And none we thought, in all the world were happier than we.
Our cattle browsed the summer hills, amid the blue-grass deep,
And all the shady bottom-lands were snowy with our sheep;
'Twas like a tale of fairy lore, the life that we lived then,

When I was barely twenty-six, and you were
    only ten;
Love brought us peace and comfort, till there
    rose an evil star,
In the summertime of plenty, when your
    father went to war.

II.

Ah, Jennie, I remember well the day,—'twas
    late in June,
Your father he came riding home from town
    one afternoon,
And his face was pale and haggard as he
    reached the door, and threw
One arm around me, daughter, while he laid
    one hand on you;
And as my senses faltered, and I reeled in his
    embrace,
I read the fearful meaning that was written in
    his face,—
I felt it in the bounding blood that beat
    against my breast,
I needed not a spoken word,—too well I knew
    the rest;

And all that night in dreams I heard the
    tramp of marching feet,
And far away I saw the flags grow dimmer
    down the street;
'Twas long ago! but O, my heart has not out-
    grown the scar
God's finger put upon it, when your father
    went to war.

III.

Then you and I were left alone. We tried a
    year or so,
By hiring help, to scrimp along, but couldn't
    make it go;
The Spring-floods swept away the corn, the
    drouth of Summer dried
The grasses on the uplands, and we had no
    crops beside;
So we parted with the cattle that we could no
    longer keep,
We sold the only team we had, and traded off
    the sheep;
And when the winds of Autumn shook the
    pipes about the eaves,

And in the woodland hollows piled the brown
    October leaves,
When the hazel-nuts were ripening in the old
    familiar copse,
And the wild geese wedging southward, far
    above the maple-tops,
We locked the dear old farm-house up, and
    closed the pasture bar,
And moved into the village, when your father
    went to war.

IV.

Then Winter came—a dreary time—a night
    of hopes and fears,
On every hand the widows wept, and fell the
    mothers' tears—
A reign of blood and ruin! Every day some
    passing train
Brought back a load of mangled men—brought
    back the coffined slain;
And Jennie, O, my Jennie, ere the snows of
    Winter passed,
They bore your father back to us,—they
    brought him home at last;

They sent him from the frozen hills, beside
    the Tennessee,
Borne down amidst the battle, where the
    bravest love to be;
They sent him back a ruined man for life,
    alas, my child!
I turned away in agony, I raved as one grown
    wild.
But why recall the story now? The years
    have drifted far,
And we've got used to trouble, since your
    father went to war.

V.

The times have changed. We, too, have
    changed. To-night the blue and gray
Sit round their fires with lighted pipes, and
    puff their hates away,—
Sit spinning yarns about their camps, until
    the drowsy stars
Put out their light and wave "good night"
    across the twilight's bars.
Although my heart be broken, and although
    my hair be white,

And 'though the years have brought me but
    disaster in their flight,
I am wicked in my weakness, I am cruel to
    complain,
When yonder patient sufferer sits smiling at
    his pain,—
Sits crooning in the Autumn moon the bal-
    lads made to praise
The luster of his daring in the old heroic
    days,—
Sits dreaming, Jennie, dreaming, of the battle-
    fields that are
The glory of the ages, since your father went
    to war.

VI.

A little while—it won't be long, until the sol-
    diers come
And bear away their comrade to the dead-
    march of a drum,
To the green hills over yonder, where eternal
    tents are spread,
And no pensions are rejected in the domains
    of the dead;

Where justice is no jester, and where glory countersigns
The muster-rolls of freedom as the century declines;
Yes, child, to that Republic where no partisan is found,
Where the private is promoted and the potentate discrowned,
Our loved one now is journeying; and as for you and me,
It matters not,—the pottersfield our heritage may be;
The future frowns and threatens, but thank God it cannot mar
The glory that we garnered when your father went to war.

AN INVOCATION.

Spirit of Mercy! draw near me, draw near me,
Lean to me lovingly, comfort, and cheer me,—
Hope have I none, if thou deign not to hear
    me.

Spirit of Mercy! encompass me, bless me,
Close to thy bosom warm, clasp me, and press
    me,
Clothe me with meekness—of sin dispossess
    me.

Spirit of Mercy! I reach to thee, cling to thee,
All my transgressions I prayerfully bring to
    thee;—
Humbly my hands, in my weakness, I wring
    to thee.

Spirit of Mercy! uplift and uplead me,
Up-tear from my pathway the snares that im-
    pede me,
Sustain and support me, whenever the need be.

AN INVOCATION.

Spirit of Mercy! of doubt disarray me,
Dismantle my life of the lusts that dismay me,
And strengthen my soul, when temptations
    waylay me.

Spirit of Mercy! be nigh to me ever,
Assist me—inspire me to higher endeavor—
Forsake me, and frown on me, never—Oh
    never!

Spirit of Mercy! I kneel to thee, kneel to thee,
Trusting thro' darkness and discord, my weal
    to thee,—
Queen of the Angels! thy sweetness unseal to
    me.

A BALLADE OF BUSY DOCTORS.

When winter pipes in the poplar-tree,
   And soles are shod with the snow and sleet—
When sick-room doors close noiselessly,
   And doctors hurry along the street;
When the bleak north winds at the gables beat,
   And the flaky noon of the night is nigh,
And the reveler's laugh grows obsolete,
   Then Death, white Death, is a-driving by.

When the cowering sinner crooks his knee,
   At the cradle-side, in suppliance sweet,
And friends converse in a minor key,
   And doctors hurry along the street;
When Crœsus flies to his country seat,
   And castaways in the garrets cry,
And in each house is a "shape and a sheet,"
   Then Death, white Death, is a-driving by.

When the blast of the autumn blinds the
 bee,
 And the long rains fall on the ruined
 wheat,
When a glimmer of green on the pools we
 see,
 And doctors hurry along the street;
When every fellow we chance to meet
 Has a fulvous glitter in either eye,
And a weary wobble in both his feet,
 Then Death, white Death, is a-driving by.

Envoy.

When farmers ride at a furious heat,
 And doctors hurry along the street,
With brave hearts under a scowling sky,
 Then Death, white Death, is a-driving by.

GOOD-NIGHT, AND JOY BE WITH YOU ALL.

The wind blows east, the wind blows west,
    The last dead leaf is on the tree,—
Farewell the merry wine and jest,
    And all good fellows dear to me;
Those raptur'd hours with feathered feet,
    My aching heart would fain recall,—
But, ah! 'tis ours no more to meet,
    Good-night, and joy be with you all

The weary world spins 'round and 'round,
    And friends must part as friends have met;
There is no spot of hallowed ground,
    If not where friendship's board is set;
The wind blows west, the wind blows east,
    Our last bright cup is mixed with gall,—
A death-head glimmers at the feast,
    Good-night, and joy be with you all.

To-morrow comes, to-morrow goes,
    But yesterday returns no more;
We meet with these, we part with those,
    And eyes are dim, and hearts are sore;

A blinding mist obscures my sight,
　　My senses with their burden pall,—
Time halts not in his rapid flight,
　　Good-night, and joy be with you all.

SHAKESPEARE.

His soul was like a palace wrought of glass,
   Star-stained and many-sided, and full-fraught
   With all the fairest flowers of human thought,
Outspread in one immeasurable mass,—
A garden of enravishments, where pass
   The rapt creations that his fancy caught
   From realms of being hitherto unsought,
Or feebly sought, or fruitlessly, alas!
He peered through nature with a prophet's ken,
   He pierced her secrets with a poet's eye,—
   With passion, power, and high philosophy,
     He set the spirit's inner gates apart;
He stripped the shackles from the souls of men,
   And sacked the fortress of the human heart.

The perfect model of the perfect mind!
   Within the spheric fullness of his sense,
   Within his kingly soul's circumference,
The image of the universe was shrined;
In lofty utterance his tongue outlined
   The golden orb of all intelligence;
   He touched the circle of omnipotence,
Defining things no other ere defined.
God made but one! the rack of centuries,
   The rolling chariot of resistless years,
   Leaves unbedimmed the amaranth he wears,
His fame is co-eternal with the skies,
His words are fadeless as our memories,
   His influence as deathless as our tears.

THE SOLDIER OF CASTILE.

I

It was afternoon in Madrid, during Isabella's reign,
When Ristori was playing in the capital of Spain,
That Nicholas Chapado, a Castilian soldier, lay
Within a dungeon doomed to die, at breaking of the day;—
A beardless boy and beautiful, with gentle voice and eye,
For some offence of discipline, a felon's death must die;
No pleading sister's upturned face—no mother's fond appeal,
No sweetheart's eloquence could save the soldier of Castile,—
And so a black-robed bellman, as the custom was, went down
Collecting alms in all the streets and by-ways of the town,

Collecting alms to pay the priest to lift his
    voice on high,
In supplication for the soul of him who had
    to die.

II

The great Italian actress, standing at her
    window high,
Saw the ghostly bellman ringing, and she
    turned and questioned "Why?"
And when a Spanish cavalier responded with
    the tale,
The listening woman shuddered, and her
    cheeks grew chill and pale,
Then, turning from the casement, where the
    sunlight softly fell,
She saw no more the bellman, and she heard
    no more the bell;
She only saw in fancy from a dungeon bare
    and gray,
A lad led forth to slaughter, at the breaking
    of the day—
A brave boy rudely ushered from a prison's
    rime and rot,

To the sunshine of the city, for an instant, to
    be shot;
And her great heart sank within her, and her
    soul in sobs escaped,
As she thought—the mimic empress—of the
    tragedies she aped.

III

And now 'twas night in Madrid, and the
    Zarzuela shone
With oriental opulence, and splendor all its
    own;
The bended balconies above, blazed like a
    triple chain,
That belted in the beauty and the chivalry of
    Spain;
Proud Isabella from her box looked out with
    haughty grace,
While the passions of a race of kings were
    pulsing in her face;
Anon, amidst a clash of bells, and 'midst the
    crowd's acclaim,
The pale Italian sorceress before the foot-
    lights came;

A glory fell about her, as her tragic spirit
    played
On the passions of the Spaniards, in their
    royal pomp arrayed;
She tranced them with her tenderness—she
    touched them as with steel—
She broke a pathway to the coldest heart in
    old Castile.

IV.

'Twas midnight, and the play was done—the
    closing curtain fell,
And Ristori was kneeling at the feet of
    Isabelle—
Lo! the mimic queen was pleading with an
    eloquence unknown,
For Nicholas Chapado, to the queen upon the
    throne;
All motionless and silent stood the swarthy
    cavaliers,
Their bosoms wrung with pity, as they leaned
    upon their spears;
'Twas the picture of a passion—'twas a
    priestess of her art,

At the feet of Mercy kneeling, with her
    pleading lips apart;
'Twas a woman's heart appealing—'twas
    resistless as the seas,
Or the rushing North that hurtles down the
    snowy Pyrenees;
The haughty Queen was conquered—and that
    night the links of steel
Fell, broken at her bidding, from the soldier
    of Castile.

HER FEET ON THE FENDER.

I.

The winter blew chill, but the night it was white
  As the satiny sheen of the hand that I crushed,
As we sat where the bright chandelier shed its light
  On her billowy curtains and ottoman plushed;
It was middle December outside, but I swear,
  I could hear the birds sing, and could feel the Spring's splendor
Blown into my blood, from her tropical hair,
  As she teetered her tender white feet on the fender.

II.

We are wed,—and the days they have sped overhead
  Like the half-finished dreams of a lover, who lies

In the cool summer night, when the planets burn red
  Thro' the lattice that shadows his slumberless eyes;—
It is middle December,—the chandelier glows,
  And I fall to the floor in most servile surrender,—
And *she?*—Well, I tickle her baby's pink toes,
  As she smilingly sews, with her feet on the fender.

THE OLD VILLAGE DEPOT.

There stands the old station-house, out in the
 rain,
A stone's throw away from my door,
With its wind-shaken wall, and its weather-
 racked pane,
And its rickety, rat-haunted floor;
Its sashes are seamed, and its lintels are
 gashed,
With the jack-knives of twenty long years;
And the eaves, where the wings of the swal-
 lows once flashed,
Seem touched with a kinship of tears.

Old house! it looms up like a ghost in the
 gale,
And gibbers and groans in the blast,
And speaks with a weird and a weariless wail,
Of the dim, irretrievable past;
On the old dingy platform that girdles it
 'round,
The wealth of the prairie once poured,

And daily the carriage of commerce came
    down
  With the wares of the stranger aboard.

'Twas here, when our brothers went off to the
    wars,
  We blessed them and bade them adieu;
And we welcomed them, here, 'neath a banner
    of stars,
  When the terrible conflict was through;
And here where the bare-footed boys are at
    play,
  The war trumpets thundered of yore,—
And here came the coffins in ghastly array,
  Of the dear soldier-dead to our door.

'Twas here the young bride in her beauty and
    bloom,
  To her cheek felt the parting kiss press'd,
And here beat with rapture the heart of the
    groom,
  As he cradled her form on his breast;
And here in his squalor the beggar has crept,
  To shelter himself from the blast,

In the merciless midnight, and dreamed as he
    slept,
  Of the happier days of the past.

And here came the message more fleet than
    the dove,
  O'er the wavering, wandering wire,
That filled us with grief, or that thrilled us
    with love,
  As we peacefully sat by the fire;
Ah, the old station-house! it will soon tum-
    ble down,
  Its timbers are crumbling away;
But its record is writ on the heart of the
    town,
  And its glory abideth for aye.

INDIAN SUMMER.

Upon the bleak November hills
A solitary bluebird trills
His latest song,—and far along
The russet upland loudly rings
The lay the sturdy woodman sings.

Beyond the pasture's hazel edge,
From out the hollow's tangled sedge,
The quail upsprings, on whirring wings,
And down the stubble flutters fast,
Before the hunter's heartless blast.

From out a moss-grown sugar-trough,
A lonesome rabbit gallops off
Across the woods and solitudes,
That rustle to the slightest stir
Of dropping leaf and acorn-burr.

In lazy aldermanic guise
The yellow-breasted pawpaw lies,
So snugly hid the leaves amid,
That scarce a schoolboy's eager eye
Can find it as he saunters by.

In lines that waver and converge,
The puzzled wild-ducks southward surge
The live-long day,—while far away,
A circling hawk is seen to swim
Along the twilight's amber rim.

The blue-jays on the windy oak
Hold joyless jabber thro' the smoke
Of these dim days;—while faintly strays
From orchard haunts, and leafless groves,
The murmur of the patient doves.

Beyond the river's fringe of mist
The wild vines climb and intertwist
Their amorous shoots, rich hung with fruits
That froth with wine so ripe and fair
The fairies fill their flagons there.

Within the forest brown and seared,
To-day no harsher sound is heard
Than lisps of rills, and timorous trills
Of birds that seek a shelter from
The surly winter soon to come.

It were as if some sudden shock
Had stopped the wheels of Nature's clock
An instant, ere the flying year
Sent forth his trumpeters to blow
The signals of approaching snow.

O glorious Indian Summer time!
Where is the country, where the clime,
To match with this? O, land of bliss,—
O, land of love, and light and flowers!
God made it last, and made it ours.

LADY LAURA IN THE NORTH.

I

Lady Laura, in the North,
    Leaning at her lattice high,
Lingeringly looking forth,
    Saw the wild swan southward fly,—
Heard afar the clanging cranes,
    Sweeping from the fields of snow,
To the sun-lit, summer plains,
    Where the warm magnolias blow.

II

Lady Laura, looking south,
    Trembled like an aspen leaf,
While around her perfect mouth,
    Crept the early curves of grief;
All her life seemed but a ring
    Of remembrance, and regret,
As she stood there quivering
    Like a wind-swayed violet.

III

Lady Laura, lily-tall,
   Standing at her casement high,
Saw the evening shadows fall,
   Saw the wild-birds homeward fly;—
But she spake not any word,
   Staring hard against the sky,—
Never any sound she heard
   Of the loud world rolling by.

IV

Lady Laura, leaning there,
   Lonely, in a land forlorn,
Saw a child with sunny hair,
   Rise beyond the clouded corn;—
Fell her tears, like autumn rain,
   As she thought of one dark day,
And a warrior lying slain,
   On the banks of Mobile Bay.

V

Lady Laura—she is gone!
   Lonely is that lattice high,—
Still forever flies the swan,
   Still the clanging cranes go by;

In the North, a wanderer
   Clutches for a vanished hand;
Desolate idolater,—
   He can never understand.

MEADOWS OF GOLD.

Meadows of gold,—
   Rolling and reeling a-west!
Ye clasp and hold
   The milk of the world in your breast.
Ye are the nurses who clutch
The ladies of life, and touch
The lips that famish and burn,
In agony cruel and stern.

Meadows of gold,—
   Reaching and running away!
Shod with the mold,
   And crowned with the light of the day.
Ye are the chemists of earth,
The wizards who waken to birth
The violets blue, and butter-cups, too,
Under the dark and the dew.

Meadows of gold,—
   Winding and wending along,
Fair to behold,
   And merry and mellow with song.

Ye are the poets whose chimes
Are rung by the reapers–whose rhymes
Are written in windrows of grass,
By musical sickles that pass!

Meadows of gold,—
   Laughing and leaping afar!
Fast in your fold,
   Forever the beautiful are.
Ye are the Hebes who dip,
And lift from the loam to the lip,
The nectar, whose plethoric flood
Is tinted and turned into blood.

AT UNCLE REUBEN RAGAN'S.

At Uncle Reubel Ragan's!—why, the present is forgot
At the very faintest mention of the old enchanted spot;
And swifter than a swallow skimming down the dewy corn,
My memory goes laughing back to boyhood's mellow morn,—
And again I feel the breezes of the beech-woods on my cheek,
As I pass with bow and arrow by the spring-house and the creek,
And merrily wend onward to the Mecca of my joys,
To spend a day in Paradise, with Uncle Reuben's boys.

At Uncle Reuben Ragan's everything was fair and sweet,
From the blue sky bending over, to the blue grass at our feet,—
From the lisp and trill and twitter of the cat-bird and the lark,

To the whippoorwill that whistled from the dingle thro' the dark;
The days were full of riot, and the nights were full of rest
As balmy as the moonlight on the squirrel's breezy nest:—
As I plod the dim past over, and recount its keenest joys,
My bare-foot fancy wanders off with Uncle Reuben's boys.

I can hear the walnuts dropping in the pasture, as of old,
I can see the russets rounding into solid globes of gold;
I can see the bearded chestnuts clinging to the browning boughs,
In the corner of the orchard, just beyond the saddle-house;
I can hear the cider gushing from the mill, just over there,
On the slope, across the hollow, in the cool October air:—
O, I live the old life over, in my fancy, as my mind

Re-pictures and re-peoples every scene it left
    behind.

The little stream that toddled down the yard,
    and slipped away
Thro' the pasture, still is tinkling in my
    memory to-day,
And the barn that stood beyond it, seems to
    beckon to me still,
With its ever-greedy rat-traps, and its old
    red fanning mill;
And the plum-patch in the garden, and the
    tall mulberry tree,
That grew beside the milk-house, are a-calling
    back to me,—
And again the maple sugar is a-trickling off
    my tongue,
Into streams of sweeter music than my lips
    have ever sung.

Count my fingers three times over, and they
    scarce make up the years
That have vanished, like a vision, in the
    torrent of my tears,
Since the happy days of boyhood, ere the
    green earth claimed its own,

And Uncle sank to slumber in the shadow of the stone:—
Gone the many forms and faces—but a scattered few remain,
To meet us, and to greet us, at the old homestead again;
And I—well, here I'm sitting 'neath my pines in Illinois,
And drinking cider—in my dreams—with Uncle Reuben's boys.

THE NIGHT YOU QUOTED BURNS TO ME.

The winds of early autumn blew
   Across the midnight. Overhead
   A wild moon up the heavens fled,
And cut the sable vault in two;
We heard the river lap and flow,
   We turned our poet-fancies free—
My heart did all its cares forego,
   The night you quoted Burns to me.

A gray owl from a blasted limb,
   Dropped down the dark, and blundered by,
   As if a fiend with flaming eye
Fast-followed in pursuit of him;
Ah, then you crooned beneath the moon,
   A ditty weird as weird could be—
And Tam O'Shanter crossed the Doon,
   The night you quoted Burns to me.

We praised the "Lass o' Ballochmyle,"
   We talked of Mary, loved and lost,
   Until our spirits touched and crossed,
And melted into tears, the while;

We drank to "Nell," and "Bonnie Jean,"
    To "Chloris," and the "Banks o' Cree,"—
Blest hour! I keep its memory green,
    The night you quoted Burns to me.

The Wabash hills their heads low hung,
    As floating up their winding ways
    They caught the sound of "Logan Braes,"
And heard "Sweet Afton's" glory sung;
And loud the Wabash did deplore
    That no brave poet-voice had she,
To lend *her* fame, forevermore,
    The night you quoted Burns to me.

O dear, delightful autumn night,
    Forever gone beyond recall!
    Comrade, the clouds are over all,
And you—you've vanished from my sight;
Still flows the river as of yore,
    The owl still haunts the lonely tree,
And I'll forget, ah, nevermore,
    The night you quoted Burns to me.

THE MYSTERY OF BARRINGTON MEADOWS.

Over the Barrington meadows a riderless steed,
Whiter than moon-down mist, and swifter of speed
Than a skirring swallow, cleaves the shimmering light,
Ghost-like, galloping ever and on thro' the night.

Up from the Barrington meadows a cold face peers
For aye, at the stars, and the winds, and the shifting years,
While the low, perpetual sobs of a woman rim
The night with an agony vague as a dream and dim.

Over the Barrington meadows, and on to the morn
Go reeling the Bacchanal bats thro' the blasted corn,

While a blood-red poppy bends in the moon
    and pleads,
All night, for the soul of one lying stark in
    the reeds.

Down in the Barrington meadows a dolorous
    rune
Climbs up thro' the curling mist to the
    marble moon,
And ever the girdling clouds and the curdling
    airs
Are pale with the gibbering ghosts of un-
    heard prayers.

Down in the Barrington meadows a death-
    bird rings
The ominous sky with the rush of invisible
    wings,—
And sibilant sighs from the shuddering
    grasses rise
Like shrieks of the doomed, at the bars of
    Paradise.

Down in the Barrington meadows the flowers
    are nursed
In the poisonous blood-wet loam of a land
    accursed,

And rank as death is the pool at the root of
    the reed,
Where drinks each night the wraith of the
    flying steed.

Down in the Barrington meadows the snake's
    swift eyes
Are hot in the tangled sedge where the dead
    man lies;
And beetles black as the slayer's soul, disport
Over the crumbling palace where Life held
    court!

Down in the Barrington meadows a swart
    lagoon
Chafes under the guilty scowl of the pallid
    moon,
And penitent lilies, drugged with the dew
    and slime,
Quake with the conscious dread of a nameless
    crime.

But the spectral steed flies on, and the night-
    rains beat

Down on the crumpled heads of the ruined wheat,—
And strong men start, aghast, with a stifled cry,
When the wraith-like, horrible hoofs of the horse go by.

WHEN I AM OLD.

When I am old,
And pass into my dimmer days,
   To wither and repine,—
Will ever minstrel wake my praise,
   Or lisp one lay of mine,—
When my proud spirit's fires are cold,
     And I am old?

When I am old,
A rivelled, wrinkled mass of mould,
   And on my cheerless hearth,
I heed no more my prattling fold,
   Nor any sound of mirth,—
Shall I to dust go unconsoled,
     When I am old?

When I am old,
And seek no more to garner gold,
   And o'er my sightless eyes,
The lilies of the grave unfold
   Their petals to the skies,—
Shall I be slighted, scorned, cajoled,
     When I am old?

When I am old,
And, like a sear leaf on the wold,
  Tremble at every gale,
My deeds,—will they be unextolled,
  My loss, will none bewail,—
Will Peace her just rewards withhold,
  When I am old?

THE PASSING OF THE OLD YEAR.

I.

With stormy glances backward bent,
   And rivelled lips and wrinkled hands,
He steps at midnight from his tent,
   And hobbles down the frozen lands.

II.

Lear-like, he stands against the storm,
   His tattered raiments blown apart,—
His withered form no fire can warm,
   Nor thaw the life-blood at his heart.

III.

Like some grim Viking of the North
   Retreating from a plundered ship,
The gray-beard pilgrim presses forth,
   With scowling brow, and scornful lip.

IV.

In moody silence moving on,
   He melts into the moonless night,
And ere the bells ring up the dawn,
   His struggling spirit wings its flight.

AN EXTRAVAGANT SIMILE.

The prairie, like a paper, lies unfolded at my feet—
'Tis the Autumn's last edition—'tis her illustrated sheet—
"Nature's Quarterly!" I whisper, as my roving fancy reads
The "gossip" of the golden-rods, the "chit-chat" of the weeds;—
The "poems" of the meadows, lying scattered here and there,
The "stories" of the stubble, in full column everywhere,—
The "advertising" acres, and the "editorial" plots,
And the "parenthetic" fences round the "paragraphic" lots.

Each page is highly colored, and around the margin runs
A forest, like a ribbon, stained with many summer suns;—

The " picture " of a village in the middle column lies,
Whose tinted houses glimmer with at least a dozen dyes;
And sprinkled o'er the pages, everywhere, in gold and green,
The dwellings of the farmers, with their strawstacks in between;—
'Tis a holiday edition, and I cannot help but think
It was stereotyped in Heaven, and God put on the ink.

THE PIONEERS.

I

Here where the bannered corn and bristling
 wheat
  Toss their proud tresses to the rustling
   breeze;
Here where the arteries of commerce beat,
  Thro' laughing lands of luxury and ease,—
Where lazy cattle crop the summer leas,
  And singing rivers woo the golden sand;
Here where the poor man for his labor sees
  Perennial plenty rise on every hand,
We dwell—the youngest heirs of Freedom's
 holy land.

II

Where yonder marble city tops the plain,
  And shining temples in the sunset glow,
Where wealth and beauty hold perpetual
 reign,
  And busy hands the seeds of progress
   sow,—
In that same spot, a few short years ago,

The cabin of the swarthy pioneer,
In cheerless solitude, surpassing show,
   Nurtured beneath its roof the hearts that were
To build the Empire of the western hemisphere.

III

The giants of the infant world, who slew
   The dragons of the wilderness, were they;
Along the lakes and by the mountains blue,
   They burned the stubborn barriers away,
And blazed a passage for the brighter day,
   With ringing axes in the forest deep;
Their glory is our own! and I would pay
   The feeble tribute of my verse, to keep
Their hardships unforgot, while we their blessings reap.

IV

They dammed the rivers, and they built the mills,
   They trapped the beaver, and they tracked the bee;
They harvested the wild grapes on the hills,

And steeped the fragrant sassafras for tea,
Stealing their sugar from the maple tree;
  The bloodroot, mandrake, and the bittersweet,
All precious herbs, and bountiful and free,
  Outspread their healing virtues at their feet,—
Nature's apothecaries in her rude retreat.

V

For them the plum tree shed its purple fruit,
  In gleaming nuggets, 'midst the thicket's shade;
In Spring, the wild strawberry's tender shoot,
  Bediamonded with crimson jewels, made
The hollows glitter like a masquerade;
  Then Autumn with her brown nuts came at last,
Pouring her cornucopia in the glade,
  Ere surly winter blew his chilly blast
Upon the naked flats and sealed his larder fast.

VI

And then the snows came, and the squirrel slept
    Within the upper chambers of the oak;
And thro' the night the watchful rabbit leapt,
    And the wild fox within his den awoke,
The darkness buttoned 'round him like a cloak,
    And pausing, listened for the crowing cock;
Afar the wolf's howl thro' the forest broke,
    And the brusque owl sat hooting on the rock,
And preening the feathers of his antique frock.

VII

And Summer carpeted with shining flowers
    The old primeval temples, and the song
Of wild birds pierced the uninvaded bowers,
    With endless melody, when days were long,
And hearts were innocent, and hands were strong,
    And love as guileless as the feet were free;
And Eden streams, the Eden fields among,

Ran dimpling to the lakes and to the sea,
Like unwatched children in their idle revelry.

VIII

But those were troublous times, and fell
    disease
  Lurked like a demon in the stagnant
    swamp,
Amidst the shadows of the cypress trees,
  Where the dull fire-fly lit his chilly lamp,
And the sleek lizard slumbered in the damp,
  Beside the reeking serpent and the newt;
Contagion strode with no unsteady tramp,
  Beneath the roof, and plucked the heart's
    best fruit,
And draped the lonesome soul with agony
    acute.

IX

Anon, upon the sloping upland shone
  New billows of brown earth, unseen
    before,—
With, here and there, a strangely-shapen
    stone,
  Wraith-like, uprising from the tufted floor,

With reeling lines of grief engraven o'er
    Its ghastly facets, by some finger rude;
(Death laughs to scorn the legends on his
    door,
Whether within the dim wood's solitude,
Or in the gilded shrines, where giddy crowds
    intrude.)

X

Ah! there were dangers,—there were acci-
    dents
    By flood and field of which we little wot;
The tempest pitched its melancholy tents
    Above the forest, and the lightning hot
Flashed thro' the roaring, reeling oaks, and shot
    Its flaming bolts along each toppling height;
Trailing its terrors o'er the settler's cot,
    And marking in the fury of its flight,
Forsooth, a smoking track of ruin, wreck and
    blight.

XI

Death came in many forms,—the vengeful
    snake
    Unloosed its venom with unerring aim;

The burly black bear loitered in the brake,
   And nightly to the hill the panther came,
And stealthily outstretched its agile frame,
   To watch and seize the unresisting prey;
Aye, there were perils more than tongue can name,
   That compassed those old foresters,—yet they
With souls of flint, toiled on, thro' all that twilight grey.

XII

Around their huts the wily Indian crept,
   His shaft as sudden as the serpent's sting,
And many a weary mother, as she slept,
   Was startled by the war-whoop's dismal ring,
The hiss of arrow and the twang of string,
   Or the fierce tumult of the savage horde,
Beneath the wood, in their wild jargoning;
   And many a cabin by the torch was lowered,
And many a father's blood around his altar poured.

XIII

And prattling boys the rifle learned to wield,
  With fatal skill,—the pioneers' first trade,—
To them the bounding buck was forced to yield
  His life blood, in the leafy ambuscade,
Where, all unharmed, for ages he had strayed;
  Heroic boyhood! never belted knight
With dangling plume, more hardihood displayed
  In civil conflict, or in foreign fight,
Than daily marked the lives of those of whom I write.

XIV

All night within the clearing gleamed their fires,
  The dawn-lights of the splendor yet to come;
The wilderness reeled back before our sires,
  And Sharon's rose, deep-rooted in the gloom,
In virgin beauty bursted into bloom,
  And shook its fragrant petals o'er the sod;

Swift fingers sped the shuttle thro' the loom,
And Titan forms amid the dark hills trod,
In rugged splendor they, true oracles of God.

XV

With hands inured to toil, and hearts to love,
  The border prophets taught the Word divine;
In lowly chapel and sequestered grove,
  Their eloquence burned thro' the soul like wine,
And drew the evil-doer to the shrine
  Of wholesome virtue, rectitude, and grace;
They tamed the recreant with words benign,
  And brightened every hope-abandoned face,
With blessed comfortings—these Cartwrights of the race.

XVI

But they are gone,—the old plantocracy,—
  They've withered from the green-wood, one and all;
Above their dust the wind howls dolefully,
  And the last coon-skin moulders on the wall;

All, all, are gone,—and darkness like a pall,
   Steals o'er the mem'ry of the pioneers;
We drink the honey, where they quaffed the gall,
We reap the fruitage of their bitter years,
And o'er their slumbers deep, outpour the meed of tears.

XVII

Soft be their pillow in the forest old,
   And sweet the psalmody of bird and bee!
Their deeds by distant ages shall be told,
   Their virtues be transplanted o'er the sea;
Their valor built the newer heraldry,
   And shook the despot on his ancient throne,
And brought imperial armies to their knee;
   They were our sires, their glory is our own,
From sainted Washington, to brave old Daniel Boone.

TAKING IN THE HAMMOCK.

O, relic sweet of summer rest,
    What fond mementoes are you keeping
Of her, the beautiful, who pressed
    Her pretty cheek to you, while sleeping?

I see a withered rose-leaf, there,
    Among your tangles intertwisted—
And here a tress of golden hair,
    That many a patient plea resisted.

This faded ribbon round your throat,
    Is one that I had given to her,—
And here I find a crumpled note,
    The relic of a rival wooer.

Ah, Hammock, 'pon my soul, I say,
    You're like a naughty, tattling lover,
Who, when his mistress is away,
    Keeps wearilessly prating of her.

Next summer, when I hang you out
    Between the pine-tree and the maple,
You'd best be cautious, thereabout,
    And less familiar with my Mabel.

AT CHRISTMAS EVE.

I.

O wind of December!
Blow high! blow low!
Blow out of the north—blow over the snow!
Blow! Blow!
Blow out of the east—blow out of the west—
Blow over the hills by the cuckoo's nest!
Blow, O wind, as you used to blow,
In the wild, white night
Of a boy's delight,
In the Christmas time of the Long Ago.

II.

O fire of December,
Glimmer and glow!
Burn like the heart of a boy I know—
Burn! burn!
Burn till the pippins burst, and then
Burn till the pop-corn fills the pan!
Burn, O fire, till the midnight chime
Shall beckon to bed
Each golden head,
To dream the dreams of the Christmas-time.

THE OLD MAJOR SPEAKS.

I.

Long, long, has been the journey, but the end is drawing near,
We started out at dawn, good wife, and now the dusk is here;
Long, long, has been the journey that our weary feet have made,
And the hopes we held the dearest, at the dawning, have decayed;
A storm came up the valley, as we crossed the Great Divide,
And two who traveled with us, then, fell stricken at our side,—
Fell, shivered in the blast of death, that round us blew and beat,—
Fell, where their bleeding bodies paved the path for Freedom's feet—
And when at last the storm was past, and all the sky grew fair,
We found the channels on our cheeks, the silver in our hair.

II.

But dry your tears, my own good wife! loop up your locks of gray,
And slip the glasses off your eyes, and cheat the years, to-day,—
For tho' the snow be on the roof, the frost be on the pane,
Some blossoms of the early spring within our hearts remain;
Still on these bleak December boughs, fast falling to decay,
In fancy I can see, to-night, again the blooms of May,—
Can hear the robin fluting on the old familiar tree,
The babble of the brook below—the bluster of the bee—
Can see the lilac blushing still, beside the garden walk,
And hear the jewelled humming-bird upon the hollyhock.

III.

Tho' long has been the journey, wife, that we have had to go,

The skies are bright above us, *now*—the winds no longer blow,—
Across the valley, yonder, I can see the open sea,
Where the ships are sailing outward to our "ain countree,"—
I can hear the sailors singing—I can see the crowded shore,
Where the signal lights are burning, and the banners blowing o'er;
We are listed for the voyage,—soon we'll reach the harbor-gate,
Where the boats come up to anchor, and we wont have long to wait,—
And when the Captain calls us, be it dark, or be it light,
We'll climb aboard the stately ship, and bid the world, "*Good-night.*"

A GARLAND FOR THE DEAD.

Dumb be the bugle and the drum,
    And light the footsteps o'er the brave;
'Tis not in festal throng we come,
    With lips that laugh, and plumes that wave;
Nay! nay! a holier task is ours,
Love writes his elegy with flowers.

When May drops down the rolling year,
    And lightly leads her choral train,
We turn with loving homage here,
    To strew these tokens o'er the slain—
O'er those who perished when the tide
Of wild war swept the country wide.

Each rounded fortress at our feet
    Enwraps a hero's patriot fire,—
Long since that heart has ceased to beat,
    That valiant spirit to aspire;
Nor sabre's clang, nor cannon's roar,
Shall break the warrior's slumber more.

Among the tombs we idly stray,
   Our souls with mournful memories rife,
Till almost in the glare of day,
   Those wasted comrades spring to life;
And here, amidst the fields and flowers,
We seem to clasp dead hands in ours.

Nor here alone does memory trace
   Her sable lines of dumb despair,—
On many a distant battle-place,
   Their eyeless sockets upward stare,
Where never weeping kindred come,
With bended head and muffled drum.

They sleep beside the Tennessee,
   By Donelson's old ruined fort;
In Sherman's pathway to the sea
   The pale battalions hold their court;
From Franklin, Shiloh, Malvern Hill,
They answer to the death-roll still.

On Mission Ridge the wild birds chant
   Above the gray blouse and the blue,
And where the gallant hosts of Grant
   Stormed Vicksburg, there the dead are, too;

Their records, writ with shot and shell,
Show how they fought, and how they fell.

They rest by Libby's ruined pile,
   From Georgia's hell their wraiths arise;
They sleep beside the dark Belle Isle,
   And 'neath the Carolina skies,—
A shadowy band and desolate,
Whose graves no hand may decorate.

By dim lagoons where serpents trail,
   And seldom human footsteps pass;
Their bones are whitening in the gale,
   And glistening in the tangled grass;
Their guns still mould'ring in their grasp,
The friends that felt their parting clasp.

     *   *   *   *   *

The pyramids by Cheops built
   At length shall crumble and decay,
But never blood for Freedom spilt
   The tears of heaven shall wash away;
A sacred symbol shall it be
Of those who died for liberty.

THE FOOLISH MARINERS.

(For the Children.)

They set us afloat in a willow boat,
    Upon a northern sea,
And we drifted on thro' dusk and dawn,
    As merry as men could be;
The air was white to left and right,
    And white was the air before,
But behind our bark the world was dark,
    And we heard the kraken roar.

As we passed the lair of the Polar bear,
    We called aloud to him,
And he came to the door, and sniffed and
    swore,
    And stroked his eyebrows grim,—
Then buttoned his coat about his throat,
    And galloped along in our train,
So far and fast, that he froze at last,
    And never got home again.

We shook our fist at the fog and mist,
    All under the Arctic Zone,

And sailed away, from day to day,
   So jolly, and cold, and lone,—
So jolly and cold, so free and bold,
   A curious sight were we,
A-sailing away from day to day,
   Upon the northern sea.

And round about and in and out,
   Wherever the breeze up-blew,
With shout and song we swept along,
   An hundred summers through;
Yet day by day we all turned gray,
   And skinny, and grim, and wild,—
But the captain he, and the mate and me,
   We sat, and smiled, and smiled.

I smiled at the mate, and the captain, straight,
   He grinned at the mate and me,
And to lessen the weight we killed and ate
   The rest of the crew, you see;
Then the captain he grew fond of me,
   And I grew fond of the mate,
And all together we killed each other,
   And ate, and ate, and ate.

Now, harken here, my children dear,
   If ever you put to sea,
Remember the mate, and the captain's fate,
   And the end that came to me;
Bad luck to the day we sailed away,
   In search of the Northern Pole,—
My skeleton lies under Arctic skies,
   And the good Lord has my soul.

SONNETS AND RONDEAUX

TO A SLEEPING BOY.

Ah, little dreamer! stealing from the day,
   The golden keystone of the arching hours,
   To lay thy drowsy head among the flowers,
And down Lethean waters sail away!
The wind is in thy ringlets, boy, and they,
   In flossy tumult, fall in fairy showers
   Around thy cheek, and all thy childish
      powers
Are chained in sleep, beneath the sun's
   bright ray.
The beetle, droning in the apple tree,
   Thy mate is, and the whistling bobolink
Pipes half his sweetest roundelays to thee;
Sleep, little truant, in the singing grass!
   The days will wither, and the years will
      shrink,
And all too soon thy rosy dreams will pass.

A NIGHT IN JUNE.

Upon the cooling summer grass the dark
   Falls lightly, and the panting violet
   Uplifts its purple lip and lash of jet,
To sip the slow-descending dews. The lark
Is softly sleeping, pillowed in an ark
   Of sighing grasses, like some old regret
   Couched in the bosom of an anchoret,
Amid dead loves that rattle stiff and stark.
The crooked moon is peering thro' the pines,
   And checkering the lawn with leaves of light,
   And belting all the dim fields with broad lines,
   That stretch like silver ribbons through the night;
Stars on the grass, and fire-flies on the vines,
   And sorrow in the breast of every wight.

WHEN I COME HOME.

When I come home, my labors through,
Between the day-fall and the dew,
   There comes a sound of nimble feet
   Swift-flying down the path to meet
My own—with laughter and halloo.

The cares that day by day accrue,
Turn backward and no more pursue,—
   Turn back from this, my welcome sweet,
      When I come home.

If I, beyond the welkin blue,
Shall e'er go thither to renew
   My life so frail and incomplete—
   I only hope some boy will greet
Me there—just as my *own* boys do,
      When I come home.

AT MILKING TIME.

At milking time, when shadows climb
The pasture-bars, and sheep bells chime
   High up along the sunset hill,—
   'Tis sweet to wander where we will,
And take no thought of care or time.

The heart of boyhood in its prime
Lights up with joy the cheek of grime,
   When katydids come out and trill,
      At milking time.

There's not in any land or clime,
An hour so sacred, so sublime,
   As that when patient kine distill
   The wines of life, in many a rill
Of rippling and resilient rhyme,
      At milking time.

OCTOBER.

Upon the dreamy upland aureoled,
  I saw the sombre artist, Autumn, stand,
  Ghostlike, against the dim and shadowy land,
Limning the hills with purple and with gold;
And while I gazed a mighty mist uprolled,
  As at the touch of some enchanter's wand,—
  And all the woods by sudden winds were fanned,
And darkness fell upon the amber wold.
Out of the frosty north, like Indian arrows,
  In never-falt'ring flight, the wild ducks flew;
And from the windy fields the summer sparrows
  Reluctantly their feathery tribes withdrew,—-
As from the heart the hopes of manhood fly,
When the sad winter of old age draws nigh.

NOVEMBER.

Deep lie the shadows on the russet slopes,
   Loud blows the wind and shrilly falls the
      hail;
   The tangled sedge-grass closes o'er the
      quail,
And on the withered hill the woodchuck
      mopes,
A dusky image of disastered hopes,
   Against whose roof the ruthless storms
      prevail;—
November! and the farmer hunts the flail,
And puny Autumn poets seek for tropes.
Alack-a-day! that Nature e'er should robe her
   Glorious form in gloomy garbs like these;
Alas! the faded splendor of October,
   The summer gone, and its Arcadian ease;
The lengthened year is glimmering to its
      close,
Mid piping tempests, and descending snows.

WHERE WILLIE WAS.

Where Willie was, the daylight dies,
And deathlike silence overlies
   The greensward and the garden, where
   His baby feet, once brown and bare,
Went pattering under summer skies.

Now stilled for aye the childish cries,
And hushed the tender lullabies
   A mother sang, at twilight, there,
      Where Willie was.

And I—I marvel if those eyes,
Unsealed in yonder Paradise,
   Look, ever, down the shining stair
   Upon the little empty chair,
And scattered playthings that we prize,
      Where Willie was.

IN DAYS TO COME.

(TO J. W. R.)

In days to come, when you and I
Wax faint and frail, and heartfires die,
   And tinkling rhymes no more obey
   The wooing lips of yesterday,
How slowly will the hours go by.

When we have drained our song-cups dry,
My comrade, shall we sit and sigh,
   Childlike, o'er joys too sweet to stay,
      In days to come?

Nay! nay! we'll give old time the lie,
And, thatched with three score years, we'll try
   A rondeau or a roundelay,
   As long as any lute-string may,
To our light touches, make reply—
      In days to come.

CHRISTMAS MORNING.

And now the good St. Nick is come and gone,
   And many a fluffy head bursts into flower,
   Above the blanket, at the twilight hour,
With darting eyes that dip into the dawn,
Seeking the cheery chimney-jamb, whereon
   The pouting stocking, like some toppling tower,
   Breaks with its weight, and splits into a shower
Of broken rainbows, round a tropic zone.
The sun climbs up and on! the merry chime
   Of mellow sleigh-bells tinkle o'er the snow;
Each crimpled shrub is rimpled up with rime,
   And from the eaves the long icicles grow,
Till night steals on, and moonbeams through the trees
Kiss down our lids to pleasant memories.

DOOM.

There is a legend by the Norsemen told,
   How Odin to each field of battle sends
   His priestess, Valkyr, at whose finger-ends
The spools of destiny are all unrolled;
Pallid as Parian marble and as cold,
   She passes where the thickest carnage trends,
   Ambassadress of doom to foes and friends,
Marking for speedy death the strong and bold.
So, in the silent underlands of life,
   Concealed amidst the sunshine, airy forms
   And subtle, sit perpetually and spin
The tangled toils that trip us in the strife,—
   They braid the lightning and unbind the storms,
   And ope the gates for death to enter in.

RONDEAUX OF REMEMBRANCE.

In airy halls they dwell, to-day,
These friends of ours!—On every spray,
   Again the blooms of summer cling,
   Again the bonnie blue-birds sing,
But they come not, for aye and aye.

We hear their voices far away,
Beyond the night, beyond the day,
   Beyond the sound of sorrowing,
      In airy halls.

They lived—they loved—the Blue and Gray,
They fought as brave men fight, alway,—
   They fell—God knows their suffering!
   God knows we wept when Death's fell sting
First set their stormy souls astray,
      In airy halls.

They're now at rest! No bugle's bray,
No sound of flute, no virelay,
   No murmur of returning spring,
   Nor any wild-bird's caroling,
Can wake them more—ah, well-a-day!

Beneath the loving light of May,
Where we our tender tributes pay,
  In tears of sweet remembering,
    They're now at rest.

We sigh—we sing in strains that say,
To them whose brows are bound with bay,
  "God bless you!" while we wreathe and ring
  Their tombs with amaranth. A king
For such a death might pray, but they—
    They're now at rest.

DR. JOHN A. WARDER.

(ARBORICULTURIST.)

His was the gentle spirit of the woods,
   The genius of the tongueless mysteries,
   Eternally that dwell within the trees,
The flowers, the grasses, and the bursting
      buds;
A member of their secret brotherhoods,
   He caught the everlasting symphonies
   Of all the lute-lipped leaves. He held the
      keys
Of Nature's variant moods and solitudes.
A Druid gray, his loving life-blood leapt
   In transport tremulous, beneath the power
Of beauty and of symmetry that slept
   Within the petals of the frailest flower;
Sweetest of all the songless bards! he kept
   His great soul stainless in his Eden-bower.

A BLUEBIRD IN JANUARY.

A ballet-dancer in a church yard, thou,—
   A jester in a charnel-house—a gleam
   Of sunlight falling on a frozen stream—
A sapphire shining on an Ethiop's brow!
O, bluebird lone, perched on that withered bough,
   Come whistle round our doorway, till we dream
   That winter days are over, and the beam
Of jocund summer glitters on the plow.
The mellow ditties of thy dapper throat
   Fill all the icy air with phantom Springs,—
   And plumaged pipers with a rush of wings,
Seem swarming hither at thy venturous note;
   But, ah, brave minstrel, bleaker days must be
   Ere blooms the buttercup and hums the bee.

COULD SHE BUT KNOW?

Could she but know the love that stings
My panting heart, and beats its wings
   Against my lips, in dire distress,
   I wonder if the sorceress
Would deign to soothe its clamorings?

Could she but know the secret springs
That feed my soul with sufferings,
   Would she the bitter pangs make less,—
      Could she but know?

Could she but know the doubt that flings
Its shadow o'er my heart, and brings
   Destroying nights of sleeplessness,—
   O would her pitying lips express
One word,—and end my torturings,
      Could she but know?

COULD LOVE DO MORE.

Could love do more? He laid his hand
Upon the battle-axe and brand,
   And through the conflict's fire and smoke,
   Flashed swift and keen his sabre stroke,
At her imperious command.

He won renown in all the land,
For her sweet sake,—that he might stand,
   Triumphant, and her love invoke—
      Could love do more?

Alas! she scorned him. Pale and bland,
He turned away. Upon the strand,
   They found him when the morning broke,
   With blood upon his brow and cloak,
And only *she* could understand:—
      Could love do more?

MY FAVORITE POEM.

It is a little volume, velvet-faced,
   Lettered with blue, and flecked with pink and white,
With flowers of fancy daintily bedight,
On leaves of lilied purity, and graced
With quaint designs, inwrought and interlaced,
   That touch the critic sense with keen delight,—
   And on the first page, Love's own copyright,
In lines of beauty delicately traced.
A miracle of poetry! Each day
   I re-peruse it, for within it lies
A dream of joy that charms my cares away,
   And opes for me the gates of Paradise;
Nor can I from its sweet enchantment stray,
   The wondrous epic of *my baby's eyes.*

DEATH,—WHAT IS IT?

It is a peaceful end of all desire,
    An end of dreaming, and an end of song,—
    A happy winding-up of right and wrong,
A quiet quenching of the vital fire;
A shadow lying on a broken lyre,—
    A beggar's holiday,—a twilight long,—
    A landing-place where weary pilgrims throng,
A tranquil terminus of ways that tire.
Death is a respite from each vain regret,
    It drops the curtain, it concludes the play,
    It turns the lights out, and it leads the way,
When o'er the house-tops all the stars have set;
    Death is the epilogue to which we list,
    Just as the tired audience is dismissed.